10/18/01

PARVIN DARABI
AND ROMIN P. THOMSON

Rage Against the Veil

The Courageous Life
and Death of an Islamic
Dissident

Prometheus Books

59 John Glenn Drive
Amherst, New York 14228-2197

Published 1999 by Prometheus Books

03 02 01 00 99   5 4 3 2 1

Library of Congress Cataloging-in-Publication Data

Darabi, Parvin.
   [Du wolltest fliegen. English]
   Rage against the veil : the courageous life and death of an Islamic dissident /
Parvin Darabi and Romin P. Thomson.
      p.   cm.
   Includes index.
   ISBN 1–57392–682–5 (alk. paper)
   1. Darabi, Parvin. 2. Women's rights—Iran. 3. Women's rights—Religious
aspects—Islam. 4. Women—Legal status, laws, etc.—Iran. I. Thomson, Romin P.
II. Title.
HQ1735.2.Z75D37   1999
323.3´4´092—dc21   98–54854
[B]
                                               CIP

Printed in the United States of America on acid-free paper

For Homa.

How happy is a bird who has never seen a cage?
Even happier is the one who has fled the cage.
They have broken our wings and
opened the doors of the cage.

—Sadegh Sarmad

Contents

Acknowledgments

The authors wish to thank Helmut Feller for his contributions and expert advice. Likewise sincere thanks are extended to the late Gustav Luebbe, Anja Kleinlein and Peter Molden without their encouragement this project would not have been realized. Our gratitude includes Betty Mahmoody, our relatives and friends, as well as Reiner D. Meier and we thank them for their assistance and that we have been allowed to stir up their memories with our questions.

To our mother and grandmother we would like to show our sincere respect and assure her of our deep understanding of her ordeal and its circumstances. We share with her the grief of Homa's too early departure.

Chapter 1

Freedom Flames

February 22, 1994

When my uncle Hossain called from Iran to tell me what had happened, my sister had already been buried. It was early and the phone woke me. Half asleep, I picked up the receiver and heard his voice tremble.

"Parvin?"

"Hossain, what is it?"

"Sweetheart, it's Homa, she—" He wheezed softly and paused.

"What do you mean?!" I sat up quickly. "What's happened to Homa?! Is she all right?" I had been worried about her for several months. "Is she dead?!" I was screaming. Over the static, I heard him crying. I also heard my mother in the background. She was hysterical. They were bawling over the phone and I didn't understand why.

I was bracing myself for awful news. I knew my sister was very depressed and disappointed with her life in Iran. I feared the worst and kept asking my uncle, but he wouldn't stop crying. I was terrified and my heart sank when I tried to imagine what it could have been. I just kept asking, "Is she dead?! Is she dead?!"

Finally he gained his composure long enough to say "Yes." And then he began crying again.

As my head turned toward my husband, I started to cry. I felt myself sliding off the edge of the bed and falling down on the floor. I sat there, hunched over, holding the phone against my ear and my hand over my mouth. Tears rolled down my face and I felt paralyzed.

My uncle's voice broke repeatedly as he told me how Homa and my mother had spent the day together before she died. He told me they'd had lunch together at Homa's house. He said my mother was napping when Homa quietly left. She walked to her car and drove to the northern part of Tehran, an area called Tajrish.

My uncle fought to keep his composure between every word. "She must have stopped somewhere to buy the gasoline," he said.

"I don't understand!" I wasn't thinking. I had no idea.

"Oh sweetheart! It's awful. I don't want to tell you. It's your sister; it shouldn't be this way!"

"What happened to her?!"

He didn't answer me for a while. He only wept. I could tell he was trying to explain, but each time he started to speak his voice would cripple and he would cry more. It was hard to listen to him. He sounded helpless.

"Just wait," I told him. "I'll wait for you. You can tell me when you're ready."

He cried a while longer and finally caught his breath long enough to explain. "Sweetheart, your sister drove to Tajrish. She went there with the gasoline and she burned herself. She burned in front of hundreds of people. She burned like that—with everyone watching."

I heard him, but I struggled to comprehend the things he was telling me. It was as though he was speaking too quickly for me to hear the words. As he spoke, what he was telling me would sink in, and then the horrible sadness I felt would overcome me and I wouldn't be able to hear him anymore. The realization of what he was telling me fell onto me in waves of immense pain.

I couldn't listen anymore. When he called, I only wanted to know if she was dead. That, to me, was the worst-case scenario. I thought there would be nothing that he could say to me about my sister that could be more awful. I was naive.

I asked to talk to my mother. She came on the line and her voice was hoarse. I could tell she'd been crying for a long time. She was devastated. She couldn't speak without sobbing and she only repeated the same phrases. All she could talk about was being with Homa in the morning, before she killed herself. She kept telling me about their lunch and how Homa seemed relaxed while they ate together. But when she woke from her nap, she worried because she couldn't find Homa in the house.

Then she cried and told me about all the places she had called to try and find her. She said Homa's husband called in the evening. As she continued, her voice grew louder and she continued to weep. She said she'd rushed quickly to get to the hospital, but by the time she arrived the doctors had already given up on Homa.

She told this story several times and I couldn't stop her. I only listened and waited for her to calm down. When she was too grieved to continue, she gave the phone to my grandmother, who seemed to be suffering even more. Grandma cried and told me about having been proud to reach the age of eighty-six without ever burying a child or a grandchild. I tried to comfort her, but there was little I could do from so far away.

I listened for a while longer and then I put the phone down. It was an awful moment. I felt a tremendous sadness within me. My husband was awakened by the conversation and he wanted to know what happened. I told him, and as I talked, the depth of the tragedy began to unfold. I started to realize that my sister was gone forever. The pain grew and I cried violently. He was also upset, but he didn't say anything. He looked after me for the rest of the morning.

The news of my sister's death was a tremendous shock. She had been one of the most prominent child psychiatrists in Iran. She was married and had brought two successful, ambitious daughters into the world. She was licensed to practice medicine in Iran, and in forty-nine states in the United States.

She was the first Iranian ever to be accepted to the American Board of Psychiatry and Neurology. She established the first clinic in Iran dedicated to treating children suffering from mental disorders that, until then, were thought to be incurable. She quickly established herself as a premier psychiatrist in Iran. She taught at the University of Tehran, worked at its hospital, and managed her own private practice.

However, her life was haunted by the fact that she had no real home. The United States was very good to her in the years she lived here, but it was never able to replace the small neighborhoods she grew up with in Iran. A sense of obligation—that she must do something to help the nation she was raised in—attached her to Iran.

But, Iran did nothing to welcome her or to appreciate her. She was mired in a society that placed little value on the rights of women. No matter what she did or who she became in Iran, she was destined to always be no more than a woman in a country in which being a woman meant little.

Throughout her life, she fought to change the inequities and reverse the injustices faced by all people in Iran. In the end, however, obstacles proved too powerful for her to overcome. Those obstacles took the form of a husband that seemed apathetic to his wife, a government that treated her with disrespect, and a combination of influences that affected her life from the day she was born until the day she died.

The day of my uncle's call, I eventually made my way out of bed and called an Iranian newspaper and asked the editor to place an announcement about my sister's death. To his question of how she died, I told him to write "unexpectedly."

In the afternoon, the editor called back to ask me if my sister was the same person who had set herself on fire in Tehran in opposition to what he called "the oppressive regime of the Islamic Republic."

I told him that I did not know the details of her death.

He explained that his newspaper had received the news through the BBC of London and the Israeli News Radio.

After that, I had to know what really happened. I called my uncle, and the story of my sister's death began to take on immense proportions.

My uncle said he didn't know what happened because no one in the family was near my sister at the time. But, he said, several people had seen her in Tajrish, a suburb of Tehran. She left her car with the gasoline in hand and headed to the public square. Several people took notice of her as she removed the scarf from her head. In the Islamic Republic she could have been arrested and beaten for such behavior. In a way I wished that she had been arrested. Perhaps she would have survived the beating.

Witnesses said she wandered through crowds of people shouting slogans in every direction. She kept screaming, "Death to tyranny! Long live freedom! Long live Iran!" Several people approached her and pleaded with her to cover herself and to stop acting out. She refused.

Eventually, she stopped walking and removed her coat. She sat down on the pavement, tipped the can onto herself, and began to soak the lower part of her body with gasoline. She poured quickly, but took the time to let the liquid soak into her skin. People started to notice what she was doing and they moved away from her.

She made sure the gas permeated her lower body because she knew that a body could burn from above the waistline and live, but that she could not survive without kidneys or a bladder. When she was done with the can she set it aside and faced the crowd that was forming around her. She stood up and shouted each slogan one final time.

People were silent. They were awestruck. When she ignited the match, she was immediately engulfed in flames. For a few moments she bore the pain quietly and remained on her feet. In a matter of seconds, however, her head fell backward and she released an enormous shriek. Quickly, she collapsed to the ground on her stomach. Her head and torso scratched against the pavement as she used her arms to lift her torso so that the flames would not be smothered. The effort caused her to slide forward while she burned. Tears poured from her eyes and she continued to cry out.

The crowd backed away from her in a panic with people slamming into each other in disorganized waves. Someone had found a water hose nearby and used it to put out the flames. This only worsened matters for Homa because the water caused much of her skin to blister severely on impact.

When the fire was finally extinguished, Homa's small body lay on the pavement black from ash and moist from water. She tried slowly to position herself on the ground in the least painful manner. At times, she had to give up the attempt and let her head fall helplessly against the ground while she absorbed the pain, and until she regained the strength to move again.

She was dying there on the ground in front of everyone. Some people had gone for help and still others stood by and viewed the spectacle. A young woman in the crowd recognized her and realized that Homa's sister-in-law, Laleh, lived nearby. She ran to find her.

She told Laleh that Homa had set herself on fire. Laleh rushed to the scene, but by this time Homa's half-burned body was so charred that she could not recognize the face. The two of them stood in front of Homa and Laleh told the woman that this person could not be a part of her family.

Homa heard them and called to Laleh, "Laleh, she is right." Her voice was muffled and liquid spat from her mouth as she talked. "Can't you see? It's me, Homa. I am Homa."

The fire was out and an ambulance had come, but Homa's lower body had burned beyond repair. When Laleh heard Homa's voice, she was shocked. She ran home and called Mohsen, Homa's husband, and our mother.

Homa was brought to the closest hospital, but there was nothing they could do. The doctors knew that Homa would die; the only question was how soon it would happen. Any other patient in the same situation would probably have been left alone to die in a hospital bed or a cot in front of everyone else in the hospital. However, because she was a doctor, they moved her uptown, to the nicer Arad Hospital and gave her a private room.

She was given enough medicine to kill the pain. Her wounds were wrapped with cotton bandages. The damage had been done and so she was left alone with family and a nurse that had once worked for her.

Under the bandages, her shriveled skin was black from the soot. There were places, too, where the skin had been completely burned off by the fire and the inside of her body was exposed. Her whole body swelled with each heartbeat as her blood cells raced futilely to heal the inflammations. With each swelling she would lose more blood, and grow colder. For now, though, she could not feel the battle going on beneath her bandages. She could talk. She could endure the pain and talk because they had given her the right drugs.

What she had to say that evening has made us all feel even more confused. There was an eerie glow to Homa. She was satisfied with herself. She was pleased to see that she'd succeeded in carrying out her plan. Her language and tone were chilling.

Someone asked her what was wrong with her but she did not answer. The family was angry and hurt. They felt that what she had done would never be forgotten. Each of them also felt as though it might have been their fault in some way. Her husband asked her if she was pleased with herself. Homa said she was.

No one in our family will ever completely understand why she responded that way. Perhaps she felt that she had ended years of hopelessness with a feeling of accomplishment. Maybe she thought she would no longer be the "caged bird" she pitied throughout her life.

She died with only her nurse present, at two in the morning. The family had left earlier with the hope that she might be there in the morning when they returned. Instead, she was buried that same day, at nine a.m. And in her own words, she would no longer "have to watch the brutality of mankind toward one another and especially to women and children."

There are no clear answers to why my sister took her life in front of so many. Some may wish to think that this was the tragic end of a sick person, but I don't believe that. That is why I wish to tell her story. I want to mourn the memory of Homa Darabi and to use what I remember about her to find the threads with which the fabric of her final days was woven.

Chapter 2

Horror Scenes of a Marriage

I keep thinking about that final scene and my sister lying helplessly on a hospital bed with her small charred body wrapped in white bandages. They wrapped her face so that her eyes and mouth could peer out of small gaps between the gauze.

It was ironic because she left this world under the same conditions in which she was brought into it. She was born prematurely and her body was underdeveloped. In fact, her skin was yellow. They could not find clothing small enough for their child, so our parents wrapped her in cotton bandages to keep her warm. They insulated her with the bandages and placed her in a small shoe box where she spent the first two months of her life.

When she was dying, our mother looked at her daughter's closed eyes and saw the same face that had laid beneath her fifty-four years earlier.

At that time, the doctors were certain that Homa would never survive. They insisted that the baby would not be able to keep herself warm and that it would only be a matter of time before the worst happened. Ignoring their pessimism, our parents took their daughter home, wrapped her up, and placed her in her box and waited for her to grow older.

In those days, the only heat in our home came from something we called the *korsi*. It was a wooden apparatus that stood about half a meter high and rested on four wooden legs. We kept the *korsi* in the middle of our living room and surrounded it with mattresses. Coal burned in a small stove at the base of the *korsi*. This stove was called the *mangal*. The heat generated by the *mangal* was insulated by a blanket that covered the *korsi* and the mattresses around it.

Usually the fire would die out overnight and we had to start a new one in the morning. When our parents brought Homa home, though, our father kept the fire going continually for two months. He never slept more than a few hours at a time to insure that the fire did not die out.

It was the *korsi* that kept Homa alive during the initial months of her life. It was like an incubator for her tiny body. They say she did not cry much as a newborn. She only groaned and coughed quietly. I can only imagine the muffled sound of this uncomfortable baby.

Our parents cared for Homa diligently for several months. It was considered a minor miracle that she survived, but she never grew out of that initial tinniness. As if starting a step behind, she remained small-boned and light her entire life.

Looking back, I think it's easy to understand why Homa was born prematurely. I believe it had something to do with our mother's age. She married very young.

Her given name was Eshrat. Eshrat in Farsi means "the love of life." There could be no name less appropriate for this woman. She has had a traumatic life in which she has found very few things to love. She has always had a dark side to her personality. I believe her dissatisfaction with her life began the day she was married.

She has told us the story of her wedding many times. On a cool morning in April 1937, she was at school, in Tehran, with her friends. She said the class was silent at the time, because all the students were reading their books quietly. The silence made the event more embarrassing. While she read, somebody knocked on the door of the classroom. She lifted her head to see who was knocking. But for a while she couldn't tell because the teacher did not open the door wide enough to let the visitor in.

The teacher spoke with the person outside for a while. By this time, most of the other students were trying to see what was happening outside. They all waited silently until the teacher pulled away from the door and looked back toward the classroom. She was staring at our mother, and she smiled proudly.

Our mother watched her teacher walk away from the door and come toward her seat. And when she leaned to the side, she saw who was standing outside.

The teacher spoke loudly to our mother, breaking the silence that had dominated the room. "Eshrat, stand up. Take your books. Your mother is here and it's time for you to go." She was still smiling but spoke firmly, as a sergeant addressing soldiers before battle.

Our mother did what her teacher said, but she did not understand why she was being told to leave. It would have been inappropriate for her to ask, so she packed her things and walked out of the classroom, wondering why the whole time. It was the last day she would spend in school.

After leaving the schoolhouse, our mother walked with her mother through the city until they came to a beautician's shop. There, she was to have her eyebrows plucked and the hair on her face removed with thread. She was then given a makeover and clothed in a white gown. Today, our mother recalls being terribly confused at the time and crying through the entire process.

A carriage brought them home. She cried the entire time while her mother tried to calm her. At home the two of them went into a room where other women were waiting.

They all came to the door when our mother arrived, and each one of them cheered loudly, congratulating her. They smiled jubilantly and nobody seemed to care that the bride-to-be was in tears. They brought her to a cushion in the center of the room and surrounded her with wedding decorations.

There was a white sheet of new fabric spread over the floor and over this was placed another sheet, handwoven from silk. A mirror and two matching kerosene lamps made of pink glass and wrapped with leaves were placed on the fabric. There was also a small *mangal,* a tray of wild rue to ward off evil spirits, and a container decorated with colorful spices. This arrangement is referred to as *sofreh aghd,* the ceremonial wedding spread.

The cushion on which they placed our mother was positioned so that it faced the holy city of Mecca. Being so young she really didn't understand what was happening. As she sat on the cushion, looking at herself in the mirror at the head of the *sofreh aghd,* she guessed what was about to occur.

This made her cry louder and she begged everyone to protect her, but no one seemed to pay attention. All the women were caught up in the festivities. The fact that the bride was a child and the groom was a grown man thirty-three years old had no effect on their jubilant condition. In truth, most of them had been married under the same conditions.

The ritual began when some of the women stretched the folded white cloth over Mother's head and another rubbed the two cone-shaped pieces of sugar together—to sweeten the life of the new couple. Another woman sewed a corner of the cloth—to sew the mother-in-law's mouth forever (a superstitious tradition).

During this, a *mullah* read the Islamic marriage vows to our mother. These vows consisted of the *mullah* asking our mother for permission to marry her to our father. To compensate, the *mullah* stated the groom's offer, which included a copy of the Koran, a mirror, a set of lamps, and two hundred tuman, called *mehryeh.* The *mehryeh* represents the price of the bride's virginity which the man is required to pay at the woman's request. However, the money is rarely actually transferred.

The *mullah* asks for the bride's permission three times. The first two times the girl is not supposed to respond, and our mother did not. The third time she had to say yes. Our mother remembers realizing what was happening and not wanting to say yes. She sat still and only cried. Her mother, frustrated, began pinching her and smacking her side to get her to speak. Our mother says she only responded to stop the pain.

After this, an older gentleman came into the room and squeezed through the female crowd. He sat down next to our mother on the cushion.

It was the first time our mother had ever seen the man she had just been married to. When she looked at him, she screamed so loud that a silence fell over the room and everyone stared straight at her.

The husband had seen his bride before, and he knew how young she was. He was prepared to deal with the moment. He took some pistachio nuts from his pocket, removed the shells, and handed them to his bride. She stopped crying and for some reason she started to like this man. He did not scare her anymore.

That night, a show was performed in the backyard. It was a traditional play that mimicked the life of a rich *mullah*. Our mother was enjoying the entertainment when one of her aunts forced her to get up and walk with her to a bedroom.

A new mattress and bed covering were spread on the floor. The woman undressed our mother and prepared her for bed. After the long day, she immediately fell asleep.

Our father, Esmaiel, came into the room only a little while later. It was customary for a husband to take his young bride's virginity as soon and as fast as possible. Without waking her, he began intercourse. This rapelike act was performed on a thirteen-year-old child while she tried to sleep. Outside, the play had ended and people were celebrating and listening to musicians play traditional songs.

Expectedly, our mother bled, and the bleeding continued long after her husband left the room. Men were expected to leave the room following their "triumph" to allow an aunt to enter the room and collect the bloody sheets. The next day the bloody sheets were to be presented to the groom's family as proof of the bride's virginity.

But with our mother, the bleeding wouldn't stop. She finally had to be taken to a doctor to prevent her from bleeding to death. She was raped many times after that night. Even today after so many years, the thought of sharing a bed with a man makes her tremble.

In retrospect, the joining of our mother and father was an awful, brutal marriage. Still, it might have been necessary. Our mother's family was poor and enjoyed little hope for upward mobility in a Third World country that couldn't escape its economic problems.

Our mother was one of four children, three of them girls. Feeding all these children on what little money our grandparents had was difficult. When they found a man who was willing to take care of one of the daughters, it was a solution that could help relieve the situation. Because he had considerable wealth, they thought they were doing our mother a great favor. Also, it was quite common for marriages to take place between couples of such different ages.

After their wedding, our father brought his wife into his home. A few months later our mother had her first menstruation. A month later, she was pregnant. Six months into the pregnancy, with her stomach well swollen, she started to bleed. It would have been a girl; the doctors found out when they removed it.

Then, she got pregnant with Homa and carried her for seven months. By the time Homa was nine months old, our mother was pregnant again, with me. I was a full-term baby and weighed eight pounds. Apparently, our mother's progression through puberty was complete by the time I was born.

Growing up as this young woman's children left a definite mark on us. We were her daughters, but somehow it didn't feel that way. At least, not in a traditional sense. We were sisters, but from the minute she learned to talk, Homa began assuming responsibility for me. As we grew older, she became a second mother to me, even though she was only eighteen months older.

I don't have many memories of my early childhood, but I always remember the story our father used to read to Homa and me while we were under the *korsi*, waiting to fall asleep.

He used to tell us a story that he read from the *Shahnameh*. The *Shahnameh* was a collection of stories written for the people of Iran by the poet Ferdosi. Our father read many stories from this book, but there was one story that Homa always insisted that he read.

This story was about a dancer who was hired by an army to work one night in a nightclub during the war. The club attracted a lot of enemy soldiers and the dancer was to perform for them. She was a gorgeous woman and every tired, hungry man who'd come in to get away from the violence for one single night was mesmerized by her routine. They all watched the woman closely and drank for hours as the night went on.

While she danced, though, she started to notice one person in the audience more than any other. Eventually, she found time to speak with him and before the end of the night, she was dancing for him and ignoring most of the others.

Eventually, the crowd grew drunk and the dancer tired. It was then that the army she was working for stormed into the club with their swords in the air. The intoxicated enemy was helpless and each one was easily beheaded.

Afterward, the dancer was devastated. She did not know she was being used as a trap. She cried for all of the enemy soldiers, and especially for the one she'd fallen in love with. It was a humiliating experience for the young girl.

Chapter 3

Dangerous Games

When Homa and I were born, we lived in a small neighborhood in north-west Tehran until about 1947. The families that lived around us were also having children. In all, there were five of us, all cousins, and all separated in age by about four years. Homa was the oldest. Next in age was myself, a boy named Hormoz, and two girls, Nahid and Heideh. Nahid and Heideh were sisters and their father died while they were still very young. Homa had a special relationship with Nahid. Nahid was partially crippled. Her left hand and the lower part of her left leg could not function. I could always tell my sister felt tremendous empathy for Nahid because of that. Whenever we were together, my sister stayed close to her.

Hormoz had also lost his father. He ended up moving in with us when Homa was about six years old. I think his mother wanted to have some kind of career for herself and so our father offered to take care of her son while she moved on.

Over time, the five of us became inseparable. Every afternoon we would run around the neighborhood together in search of things to do. Homa, being the oldest, always tried to look after the rest of us. She made sure we weren't doing anything too dangerous or getting into any serious trouble.

Homa had to be the responsible one. Our father was usually at work and he couldn't look after us. And our mothers were far too young to accept the responsibility. They spent most of their time together, cooking, preparing meals, cleaning, or just visiting with each other. As children, we were left alone.

The five of us rarely argued. Homa and I had our moments, though. I wish I could say I wasn't the cause of most of our fights, but that would not be true. The first fight I remember us getting into took place after I misplaced Homa's doll. The doll was a figurine of a small Persian girl with big beautiful eyes. Homa used to call it Shambeh. I used to take Shambeh and play with her whenever Homa wasn't around. On this afternoon, she had trouble finding the doll, and so she came to me.

"Parvin, where's Shambeh?"

"I left her behind the front door."

She had already checked there, because I usually left Shambeh behind the door. "But she's not there," she said.

"Then I don't know where she is, Homa, I left her behind the door."

Homa started to get angry and began to accuse me of being careless. "You lost my doll, Parvin! You're always losing things! First you lost your own doll and now you've lost mine, too."

Her words were harsh and made me cry. I really didn't know what had happened to Shambeh. I had left her near the front door of the house, but the door was open. I was just too young to realize that people actually stole things. I should have understood, though, because my own doll had been stolen.

Earlier that morning, while Homa and Nahid were inside our house, I had taken Shambeh outside. After a little while, Hormoz came over and asked if I wanted to go down the street and watch the *tazieh*. The *tazieh* is a religious show in which men dress up as imams and stage a short historical play on street corners.

Our mother napped in the afternoon and we always left the front door open so she wouldn't be disturbed when we came in and out of the house. I guess somebody must have seen Homa's doll and walked off with it. There was nothing we could do.

When we realized that Shambeh had been taken, I felt terrible, and Homa was crushed. She was furious, and I was crying and neither one of us knew what to do.

Growing up, we didn't have toys. Our father couldn't really afford them. In the bazaar we once saw some beautiful toy dolls in a shop window, and after that we started constantly asking our father to buy one for us. Of course, they were very expensive and hard to come by. In a country like Iran during the 1940s the necessities of life, food, and shelter were hard enough to find. At that time, parents worried about finding enough food to make dinner on any given night. Toys were not a high priority for most households and certainly not ours.

When we were children, we didn't understand that. We begged our father to buy us things he couldn't afford. Our crying must have broken his heart. He knew we didn't have toys. He'd seen us outside playing with dirt. We used to gather dirt into cone-shaped piles and then slowly rub sand off the top of the piles until someone found a strand of hair. Whoever found the first hair won the game.

Our father would come home for lunch every day and see us play. One day, he brought something for us. He was so excited to show us what he'd bought that he called us both into the living room and asked our mother to come in from the kitchen.

He didn't buy us dolls, but he did buy us everything necessary to make them. He bought just enough doll parts and materials to make two dolls, just like the ones we wanted.

It took Mother and her in-laws days to sew the dolls, but when they were finished, they were gorgeous. We were thrilled to have our own dolls, but it didn't take long for me to lose mine. Now Homa's was gone, too.

I have always had these memories in my head. And they're painful. I'll never forgive myself for losing those dolls. Our father must have spent a fortune to find the right parts, and he must have been proud to give them to us. He must have figured we would take care of them because we didn't have any other toys. And I must have let him down.

The night after Shambeh was stolen, Homa was still mad at me. She wanted to get even. We used to play hide-and-seek together around our house. When we played, Homa would blindfold me and tie my hands together before she hid. Then she would call out to me while I looked for her, and I was supposed to find her by following the sound of her voice.

Now there were some subtle rules of etiquette to this game. The blindfolded player was in a fairly vulnerable position considering the myriad of obstacles that could be found around our neighborhood. Because of those obstacles, it was always the role of the person hiding to warn the blindfolded person if she started walking into dangerous areas.

Specifically, Homa was to let me know if I ever got too close to the pond in the middle of the yard. The house we lived in was a two-story house with a big front yard. Our family lived on the first floor and another family rented the second. The head of the family on the second floor was named Ghasem Agha, which means Mr. Ghasem. Like most Iranian houses at the time, ours had two water reservoirs. One was covered by the house and had a faucet that reached out into the basement, below the steps, where we could get our drinking water. The other was located in the middle of the yard. It was used for washing clothing or watering plants. There was an old hand pump that brought water from the reservoir under the house to the pond inside the yard.

The pond was easily the most dangerous obstacle to warn people about when playing hide-and-seek, because it was very deep. But when Homa was mad at me she always found it tough to warn me when I wandered close to it.

When we played the night after I lost her doll, Homa used her voice to guide me, blindfolded, right into the water. Ghasem Agha ended up jumping in to fish me out.

In those days, I don't know how many times Homa and I fell into that pond and how many times Ghasem Agha came to help us. Looking back, we should have been more thankful to Ghasem Agha because he probably saved our lives several times. At the time, though, we were very naive. I don't think we realized what a service he was performing for us. We were young children and we had yet to learn how cruel life can be at times. I wish I could say that we stayed like that for years. Unfortunately, that youthful outlook changed abruptly.

Homa and I had never lived with a boy before. When Hormoz

lived in our house, we used to sleep in the same room. There were no beds. The three of us would sleep on mattresses that were laid out every night by our mother or the maid. In the morning, they would put the mattresses away so that the room could be used for other purposes.

On one of those nights, I didn't fall asleep right away.

I asked him, "Hormoz, are you asleep?" I think I might have awakened him because he didn't hear me right away. "Hormoz. Hormoz. Are you awake?"

He turned toward me. "What?"

And that's all I remember, specifically. I guess the two of us started exploring each other's bodies in a way children aren't supposed to. Homa was innocent, though. She had fallen asleep before I started talking to Hormoz.

Eventually, though, we wanted to take a look at her. So while she slept, we started pulling off her underwear very slowly. But when we started, our father stormed into the room and grabbed each one of us by our arms. I'm not sure how he managed to carry all three of us with only two arms, but he did. It's difficult to imagine, but he worked fast and efficiently and got all three of us out of the room in seconds.

He threw Homa and me into his own room and took Hormoz into another. Homa didn't understand what was happening. We stayed in that room and cried until we fell asleep again. Hormoz did not return. We knew he was being beaten because the sound of his screams came through the walls. It was a terrible feeling.

But the real pain came the next day. Even today, fifty years later, I can still see Hormoz's small body sitting on our porch step, with all of his belongings gathered in a bundle next to him. He was waiting for our father to take him to his grandmother's home to live with her.

Hormoz was thrown out of the family at the age of four for something I caused. Still, I never came to terms with the idea that something wrong had actually taken place. We were just children. Where was the harm?

Unfortunately, that was the last we ever saw of Hormoz. He was totally ostracized by the family. He was never brought to our gatherings. From then on, there would be only four of us left to pass the days in our neighborhood.

I felt very guilty for what had happened, but Homa took it worse. She cried for days. She knew Hormoz would not be able to have a good life with his grandmother, who was very old and very sick. As we grew older, Homa never forgot about Hormoz. He was a vivid memory that stayed with her. I think it was tough on her because she felt responsible—she expected herself to be able to keep control of us. In fact, for her, watching Hormoz leave must have been like losing a child.

It was something she never accepted. She talked about the boy incessantly, and she wanted to know what had become of him. Homa and I were both afraid to approach our father with questions. She always asked our uncle whenever our father's family had a gathering. He used to tell us that everything was fine. He would tell us about Hormoz's progress in school, but we didn't learn much more than that.

The New Year

The year Hormoz left was the first year I was old enough to witness the New Year's celebration. In Iran the most celebrated holiday of the year comes at the spring equinox, the first day of the Persian calendar. That day is surrounded by a series of events that take place the week before, and two weeks after.

Homa was my guide throughout the events that year. She knew that I'd never participated in any of the previous celebrations and she took it upon herself to see that I learned how to do things correctly. A few days before the equinox, she decided she would teach me what I needed to know to understand the rituals involved with the holiday.

She told me about an event celebrated on the last Wednesday of the year, called *Chahar-Shanbeh-Soury,* which literally translated means Wednesday's Party. For this, people from all over the neighborhood gather together to jump through a raging fire. She said the neighbors were to create a series of fires throughout the *koocheh,* or alley. People were to jump through them, one by one. As they jumped, they would always shout:

Give me your glow and give me your warmth
Take away my hatred and take away my pale skin!

Homa spent days helping me memorize this one statement. I had a hard time with it, but I really wanted the chance to jump through the fire, so I kept repeating it to myself until I had it memorized.

I went to sleep the night before the celebration filled with excitement. I couldn't wait to get my chance to jump over the fire. I had my lines memorized and my clothes picked out for the night. Everything was perfect. I was so eager, I barely slept.

And then I saw the fire.

I spent the entire night of *Chahar-Shanbeh-Soury* watching people jump through the fire, and my legs just froze. They were cold and stiff with fear. All I could do was stare at everyone else having the time of their lives around the fire. They seemed to be moving at a different speed. Everyone surrounding me was laughing and smiling ear-to-ear. I was surrounded by teeth.

No one seemed to understand what I felt. I wondered why no one else noticed these things.

It was one of the most traumatic moments of my childhood. Homa started pleading with me to take the leap over the flames.

"Parvin!" she screamed at me from the other end of the first fire. "Don't be frightened. It's easy! Just jump over. You'll make it. Look at everyone else."

But I just stood there and watched everyone else and cried. Nobody noticed my crying, though, because they were all making too much noise and having too much fun. Every time I watched someone fly over the flames, I felt my stomach drop because I was afraid they'd fall in. The trauma allowed my emotions to get the best of me.

Eventually, they ran out of brush to burn and had to stop the jumping. Homa came up to me then, and laughed. "Well, what happened to you? Why did you chicken out?"

I don't think she understood how scared I was. "I didn't know the fire would be so hot. If I jumped, I might have fallen in and burned."

"You wouldn't have fallen in the fire. Nobody ever falls in the fire. People have done this for centuries, and no one has ever fallen in the fire."

"How do you know?"

"Well, I'm fine, aren't I? I wasn't burned and I'm just a year and a half older than you. Come on now, stop crying," she said.

"I'm not crying. I'm just scared."

Now I am left with the irony of this conversation. Who could have predicted that the body of my beautiful young sister flying above a flame would one day die in such an inferno? In my mind I can still see her as a seven-year-old jumping over the flames, gracefully, like a deer over a fence.

Once I was able to relax again, Homa took my hand. "Now let's go. We have to get ready for *Ghashogh Zany*" (which is similar to the American tradition of "trick or treat").

"What's that?"

"Come with me and I'll show you." Homa really liked leading me around. She loved explaining things to someone for the first time. "You'll like this part. There's nothing to be scared of."

Homa grabbed my hand and gave me a metal bowl and spoon to carry. "Hold onto these. I'll tell you what to do with them later."

We stood outside the front door together. Soon most of the older children in our neighborhood had found us. Each of them also had a bowl and spoon.

When everyone was ready, we started walking through the *koocheh,* banging spoons against bowls, trying to get the attention of people inside their houses.

Homa showed me how to use my new tools. We both loved being allowed to make all that noise without getting into trouble.

Someone finally opened the front door. People came out of the house with all kinds of sweets for each of the children in our group.

On the eve of the equinox, more celebrations took place. It was a wild night in our neighborhood, but Homa and I fell asleep early, despite it. We were tired out by all the excitement. But before morning, our father came to wake us.

"Girls? Girls? Come on. You have to get up," our father said.

I think Homa started talking to him first. I just tried to keep sleeping. "But Daddy, it's not morning, it is still late at night."

"It doesn't matter, you can sleep later. Right now you both should get up so we can bring in the New Year."

Suddenly, Homa stood up and started to get excited. When she was first awakened, I don't think she realized it was New Year's Day. She tried to get me up, but I was stubborn. Finally she told me, "It's time for us to try on our new clothes. Mom's been hiding them for days. Now we can put them on because it is the New Year. I mean, the New Year starts now, or at least in a few minutes."

Iranians celebrate the New Year at the spring equinox, and the actual year always starts at the exact moment of the equinox. No matter what time of the day it occurs, everyone is expected to be ready to bid farewell to the old year and welcome the new one. To do this right, everyone dresses in brand new clothing just before the turn of the year.

That's how the festivities start. They go on for thirteen days and people are expected to forget any of the animosity they have for others.

Homa finally encouraged me to get out of bed. The two of us wandered into our parents' room to see our new clothes.

Mother was waiting for us. She had laid our new clothes on blankets on the floor. I'll never forget how impressed I was when I saw Homa's new outfit. Mother had made her a bright red shirt with long sleeves. There was an embroidered navy-blue vest that went over it. She also had a pleated skirt that matched the vest. At the time, I thought it was one of the most striking outfits I'd ever seen.

Her New Year's gift was beautiful. It made mine look awful. I could see my dress was made from the same material as Homa's. The leftover fabric from her outfit made a navy-blue skirt and a red shirt with short blue sleeves for me.

Almost as soon as I saw it, I started throwing a temper tantrum. I cried straight through the equinox and bothered my parents so much that they made Homa take off her pretty outfit and give it to me. I wore it for the first few hours of the New Year and never really wanted it after that. I was still jealous, though, and every time I saw Homa trying it on, I'd start crying again. Finally, our mother dressed us in identical clothing.

After we were dressed, our mother took us into the main room. We waited for our father to let us know the New Year had begun. He took a plate of cookies and went outside. After a few minutes, he returned, knocked on the door, and we ran to him.

"What did you bring us, Daddy?" we asked, excited.

"Health, prosperity, and good luck," he said. Then he handed us each a five-rial coin that he pulled from inside the Koran. We kissed him and our mother and after a while, took our clothes off and went to bed.

Chapter 4

Lectures

Homa had a lot to look forward to in the new year. It was to be her first year of school. I remember how sad I was, because they wouldn't let me start for another two years. I really struggled with that. My sister was not going to be home with me anymore. She was able to attend school and meet other children. I felt left out.

I used to walk to school every day to meet Homa and accompany her home when she was through. Occasionally, I surprised her by coming early.

"Parvin! What are you doing here?" Homa asked me once, during recess.

"Waiting for you," I told her.

"But this is only the first break; we've got more school."

"I know."

"Does Mom know you're here?"

"Yeah, I told her I was going to go to school with you."

Homa was confused. I guess she couldn't understand why I wanted to be there. "It's going to be a while before I come home for lunch."

"I know, I just want to sit here and watch you go to school."

A bell rang. Homa had to get to class. I waited for her for three hours. I got to see Homa and her friends for ten minutes, each hour, during their breaks. At noon, we all walked home for lunch.

In those days, school went for six hours each day, Saturday through Wednesday, and till noon on Thursdays. The schools were segregated. Boys and girls weren't supposed to see each other during the day. In fact, the girls were forced to start school at 8 in the morning. The boys started at 8:30. The boys left for home a half hour later than the girls, at 12:30 for lunch and 4:30 at the end of the day. The idea, of course, was that boys and girls should be separated during school and separated on their way to and from school.

Although I was too young to start school, I became very familiar with the walk. I started following Homa and carrying her books every day. I would walk with her and her friends. When we got to school, I would sit outside on the steps that led to the front door. When the lunch break started, I would walk her back home.

Sometimes, while Homa was in class, I would get hungry and walk back home to eat something. I would pick something up for Homa, too, so she could have a snack between classes. The school wasn't very far from home. It must have been less than a half-mile because I never had trouble walking there and back.

To get to the school, I had to pass through three *koochehs,* or alleys. There was a long path that ran through fields leading to the school. The *koochehs* were narrow with homes built on either side of them. The space was wide enough for cars, but they were not permitted on the *koocheh.* In the morning, a lot of people would walk through the alleys to buy food for lunch or to get to school. By mid-morning, the streets would be empty and I could walk through them alone. By then, women would be inside their home preparing lunches. Men would be at work, and most of the children would be in school.

In the center of the *koocheh* was a long gutter which brought water from the hills to the homes in the city. The gutter was called the *joob.* The *joob* was lined on both sides with dirt walkways. When my sister and I were young, there were no paved *koocheh.* In fact, only the main roads were paved. In our neighborhood, merchants used to pass through, offering fruits and vegetables to people who lived there. The merchants would come on foot, by bicycle, or with their donkeys. That was the way our mother shopped for most of our perishable foods.

Our house was the second house from the corner of the *koocheh*. Our father's parents lived in the house at the corner on the north side of the alley. Our father owned both houses and the one across from our grandparents that we used to call *hayat bozorgeh*, the big house.

An African family lived in one of the houses on our side of the *koocheh*. And even though the *koocheh* had a name, some people referred to it as "black man's *koocheh*." They could have been the only African family in the entire country. They were a nice family and liked Homa and me very much. We used to play with their grandchildren with whom we used to go to school.

The African family consisted of an old man and his four children. The oldest boy became a physician and the other son studied at the university. There were two daughters. One became a nurse and the other a teacher. The daughters never married, as long as we were neighbors. They used to complain that there were no other Africans around to marry. Everyone they knew was white.

I never understood what the old man did for a living because he always seemed to be home. Homa and I used to pass his house on the way home from her school. Sometimes he would greet us, offering candy or chewing gum. He used to tell us stories about his homeland. He'd tell us what it was like there, why they left, and how they ended up in our *koocheh*. We used to love sitting on his lap, listening to him talk about faraway places. We may have been too young, of course, to comprehend the existence of those places, and we certainly didn't understand the politics involved with his life, but he was a good story-teller and we were good listeners.

After passing his house, I'd have to walk the entire length of our *koocheh* eastward, and then north, through another *koocheh*, and finally east again before I would reach the field that led to Homa's school. The field was part of a ranch that belonged to a man named al-Agholi. Except for our father's houses and the African man's house, everything else in our neighborhood was part of al-Agholi's ranch.

In the morning, it was a beautiful walk through the field. There were wildflowers all along the path. Giant buttonwoods made it shady. The path was lined with fig trees and all kinds of berry bushes.

On the other side of the path stood the brick school building. It was one story tall with high mud and hay walls surrounding it. The school had a thick wooden door with a metal ring hanging on it. Once school started, the door would be closed. When it was closed, I couldn't see anything from outside.

During their breaks, Homa and her friends would come and open the door to see if I was still on the steps in front of the school. Most of the time, they wanted to know if I had something for them to eat.

Every day at noon, the girls walked through the streets dressed in their proper school clothing, except for one who followed her sister with a stack of books that almost outweighed her.

As soon as we made it home, I remember how Homa would immediately start running into the kitchen, peeling off her clothes and complaining to our mother about how hungry she was. She was always fragile, a delicate girl who tired easily. After she ate, she always had to take a nap before she could go back to school.

Our parents tried very hard to make her stronger. For lunch, our mother used to prepare young chicken for her. At that time, chicken was a delicacy. It was the most expensive meat in Iran. Iranian chickens were grain-fed and had little fat on them. They would be eaten when they were only two or three weeks old.

Our mother wouldn't buy grown chickens. It was cheaper to get them young, as chicks, and then raise them until they were old enough to eat. On the surface it made good sense, but in practice, having live chicks around caused discomfort, too. Homa used to become attached to them.

One of the chicks our mother brought home had unusually short legs. Homa was drawn to the bird because of its deformity. She decided to care for it as her pet. As it grew, our mother would talk about wanting to prepare it, and Homa would cry if she brought it up. That chicken lived with us for a while and grew quite big. At some point, though, our mother decided we couldn't raise it any longer. So she cooked it.

Homa was devastated. We sat down together for dinner and Homa refused to eat. At first she just stared at the chicken, which had been torn into pieces and was soaking in a rich marinade. Her gaze was solemn and frozen. The only movement on her face came in the form of tears that dropped from her eyes.

Finally, I reached over to spoon some of the chicken onto my plate. Homa's head jerked and she watched me take a wing from the dish. As I put it on my plate, my sister pulled it from my spoon and dropped it back into the sauce. She stood up and yelled at me.

"How can you do that?! What kind of an animal are you?! You're all animals!" She was bawling. She tried to pick up the dish to take it away from us, but our mother stopped her.

"You don't have to eat!" Our mother was hysterical also. She was angry because she wanted us to eat. She worked hard to prepare the meal and she didn't want Homa to refuse it and go to bed without food.

Homa didn't argue with her. She just ran to another room.

It was sad. No one could eat. Even our mother had a hard time with it. She started clearing the table, complaining the whole time about how ungrateful her daughter was.

For some reason, a lot of strange things happened involving our family and chickens. Our mother almost killed a man with live chickens once. Were it not for Homa, it might have happened. Our mother bought ten chicks from a vendor one day and by the next morning, eight of them were dead. She was furious when she found them and she knew the vendor would come by the house again that day. She waited for him all day. When he came, she called him over.

She grabbed the basket that held the two living chicks now sitting with the eight dead ones and showed them to the vendor. We saw her and stayed near to see what would happen. Our mother demanded that he refund the cost of all ten chicks.

He, of course, refused to pay, and she exploded. After pleading with the man for a while, she finally attacked him physically, beating him on the head with the two live chicks.

I couldn't believe it. My mother was beating a man in the middle of our *koocheh* with tiny chickens. I watched, stunned, but Homa rushed between the two of them and tried to stop the assault. She pulled Mother away from the man and pleaded with her. "Mom! Stop it! It's not the chickens' fault! You have to leave them alone! Please, stop!" She was screaming and crying.

But that's the way Homa was. The slightest bit of violence brought her to tears. She had a tender heart. She had ample sympathy to give. She hated me after I put her cat's tail into a matchbox just for fun, and yet she cried for days when the same cat ate one of her pet pigeons.

That sixth year was tough for Homa. She wasn't growing well and was much smaller than the other girls at school. In fact, she was smaller than I. To help, our parents made her eat a lot of liver, along with the chickens. Each week my mother would squeeze the juice out of a pile of raw liver into a glass so that Homa could drink it. She used to drink it and never complain. I wouldn't touch it. I couldn't even watch my sister swallowing the stuff. She needed it, though.

For a few months I continued following Homa to school. One day I was greeted by our father who wanted to change my habit. While I was sitting on the steps outside of Homa's school, he came to me and asked, "Sweetheart, what are you doing here?" He sat down on the steps, one level below me.

"I'm waiting for Homa."

While we talked, our father did not look at me, but he rested his hand on my knee and stared across the street. "Honey, what are you doing? Don't you get tired of sitting here day in and day out?" His voice was calm and smooth.

"No, I don't. I sit here every day and think that one day they might let me in."

"They won't do that," he said.

"Why not?"

"You're too young. They have rules. They say in two years, honey. Can't you wait two years?"

"But, I want to go to school, Daddy."

He turned to look at me when I said that and for a while he just watched me. Then he stood up and took my hand. "Come on, honey, let's go home."

"Daddy, I want to stay!" I was whining.

"I'll tell you what, sweetheart, come with me and on the way home we'll talk. I have an idea. Don't you want to hear it?"

I was hesitant, but I went with him. On the way home, though, he didn't talk much. I held his hand and we walked through the *koocheh* of our neighborhood together. Our father died in 1984, but I always feel he's still with me—that he's walking with me as he did that day. When we started to get close to our house, he finally shared his idea.

"What do you think about taking lessons from your daddy?"

I didn't answer, but I looked up at him, because I was confused.

"When I come home from work, I can give you lessons every night just like your sister's teacher. It would feel like you were going to school, and you wouldn't have to wait."

"Could you do that, Daddy?"

"If you would like me to, and if you would work hard. You'd have to stop going to school with your sister, though."

When Homa came home for lunch, she asked my mother where I was. I came out of the room to meet her, and she asked me why I didn't wait for her.

"Daddy is going to teach me at home," I told her.

"Then you'll stop coming to my school and waiting for me on the steps? Everyone wonders why you do that every day. They wonder what you do."

From that day forward, I started to learn to read and write and to understand math. I was a good student. And our father was often very tired by the time he started giving me lessons. I never let him skip, though. I used to remind him as soon as he got home to start teaching me.

When we studied, I got to be alone with him. The two of us would sit in one of the rooms and work on the floor. Homa and my mother were told not to interrupt us. Still, before we slept, our father read to Homa and me in our bedroom.

Chapter 5

An End to Sacrifices

That same year Homa and I witnessed a day we would never forget. In the morning, I was awakened by some strange noises. I got out of bed and looked out the window and was amazed by what I saw.

"Homa! You have to get up! Come over here and look at what's going on outside!"

Homa was in bed. She was slowly waking up.

"I can't believe this!" I continued. "There are two men in our yard with a lamb! They look like they're trying to tie its legs together."

Homa got up and rushed to the window.

"What are they doing?" I asked her.

"I don't know. We should ask Daddy."

The two of us quickly found our parents who were having breakfast in the other room.

"Daddy, what's happening outside?" Homa spoke. "Why are men out there with a lamb? Why are they trying to tie its legs? The lamb is on the ground and can't move!"

Father responded with a smile and started explaining. "Oh now, don't worry. Don't worry about this lamb. Today is a special day. It is *Ayd-e-Ghorboun*. We're going to sacrifice this lamb and give the meat to the needy."

"What's *Ayd-e-Ghorboun*?" Homa asked.

"It's a celebration that takes place on the anniversary of the day Abraham was to sacrifice his son to God. Before the sacrifice, a lamb was introduced and the child was saved."

"What does it mean to sacrifice?"

"To sacrifice is to make an offering to God."

"Why do we have to make an offering of an animal to God?" Homa asked.

"Well, we had a good year in our business, our family is healthy, and we have much to be thankful for. Now our religion tells us that it's time to pay our dues," he answered.

"Well, does it have to happen here? Right in our house? I can hear the poor animal crying! It's terrible." My sister was nervous.

"Well, where else?" Father answered.

But Homa only grew more nervous. She began pleading with our father. "Daddy! Don't let them kill the lamb. Please! Stop them!" She was starting to cry. "Why should we kill a lamb? It's a helpless animal! Please Daddy! Please!"

"Homa, please! Sweetheart." Now he was pleading with her. "This is part of our religion. We are doing this to thank God for being on our side."

Although our father was never a very religious man, for some reason he obeyed some of the rules. He almost always participated in the charitable rituals. That year he decided to sacrifice a lamb on *Ayd-e-Ghorboun* and so he ordered the slaughter.

Homa and I did not understand why we had to slaughter an animal. Homa wouldn't stop crying and feeling sorry for the lamb, and she kept begging our father to stop the ritual. But he had arranged for the sacrifice, and he couldn't cancel it at this point. Homa and I sat through the whole thing out in our yard, with both of our parents.

The animal's front legs were tied together and its back legs were tied together. It was on its side, on the pavement, jerking its head around, trying to get loose.

Two men walked up to the lamb. They were young and strong-looking. One man kneeled over the animal and pushed the weight of his body onto the back end of the beast. As he did this, he carefully gripped his hands around its legs.

The second man stood behind the lamb's head and reached around below its chin. He pulled its chin up so that the neck appeared to be stretched as far back as possible. In his other hand he held a heavy blade. I saw him raise the blade over the neck of the animal, but I didn't see the cutting because I couldn't watch.

When I did look back, though, they were done. They had stepped away from the lamb. It was left lying on the ground, helpless, struggling to breath without a throat. I looked to Homa. She had been watching the whole time and now her eyes were fixed on the lamb's head.

The head was laying flat in a pool of blood that was growing larger quickly. It kept lurching forward with its mouth open. The eyes were empty and stared into space. Then, after some time had passed, the animal started to fight. It continued to try to free its legs and in doing so, the entire body thrashed around.

The lamb continued to struggle, and then lay still. It would try to escape again and then rest. Eventually, the pauses grew longer, and the struggling became less energetic. Finally, it died. By this time so much blood had poured out of the lamb that the skin around its mouth appeared to change color.

Homa just stood and watched the whole thing. I missed much of the struggle, with my head burrowed into my father's stomach. He held my head and covered my ears because of the horrible sounds that came from the animal. It made no cries—I guess it couldn't because of the deep wound across its throat. But there were coughing noises and spitting sounds and the sound of the animal's limbs scraping across the ground when it struggled.

Later, most of our family came over to enjoy the fresh meat from the animal and to celebrate the holiday. When our aunts and uncles came over with their children, I forgot all about what had happened in the morning and started to play with my cousins.

There was kabob, made from the meat, and the lamb shanks were combined with beans and potatoes to make a soup called *abgoosht*.

To most, the celebration was a great success. But Homa was not a part of it. After the sacrifice, she felt ill. She went into one of the rooms to be alone. When the others arrived, she came out, but she didn't get involved in any of the day's activities. She wouldn't eat.

Our father never honored the sacrificial ritual again. I don't know if it was Homa's reaction that changed his mind about it, or if he decided it was a wrong thing to do. Maybe it was because his construction business began doing poorly. Whatever the reason, as I remember it, what little faith our father had in his religion seemed to be deteriorating as time passed.

It took Homa a long time to recover from what she'd seen at the sacrifice. For several days she couldn't keep food down and for weeks after that she wouldn't smile. She wasn't angry at anyone and she didn't mean to make anyone uncomfortable. The event just made her feel ill.

Something about that day affected our parents also. Their relationship worsened considerably over the next few years. Business was dropping off and our father was under a lot of pressure. He was more temperamental than ever, and our mother seemed too willing to antagonize him. Sometimes, I thought she wanted to fight with him.

"Parvin, what are you doing?" demanded Homa

I was standing behind the radio, staring into it. "I am trying to see if there is a man in this box."

"There is no man in the box. And that is not a box, it is a radio."

"I know it is a radio. I just want to know how it works."

"Well, you don't have to take it apart to find out."

"Then how can I find out how a radio works? I asked Daddy and he told me there is a man sitting in the box and he talks."

"And you believed him?"

"Well, not really. But I want to find out."

"It has to do with waves. The radio station in town sends out the waves and the radio receives them."

"What are waves?"

"They're like the waves in the ocean, but they're in the air."

"What?" I was confused.

By this time, we were living in the upper section of Tehran in a house on Moshtagh Street. Our home was across from an in-door/out-door cinema. In the summer, Homa and I used to crawl out onto our roof and watch the movies.

This house was very modern compared to the house we used to live in. For the first time in our lives, we had the comfort of running water, electricity, and indoor plumbing.

It was fascinating to me that a flip of a switch could shed light on complete darkness.

"Parvin! Stop it!"

"But, Homa, it's amazing. One second it is dark and the next, it's light. Isn't it great! We don't even need a lantern." I continued playing with the switch.

"I'm trying to study! I don't care about the light. Just leave it on."

"But this is incredible," I said.

"Then do it in another room! Go to the kitchen!"

"Mom gets mad!"

"Why do you have to be such a pest?!" she snapped.

"I'm not a pest!"

"Just leave me alone!"

We lived on Moshtagh Street for four years, while Homa and I were in grammar school. We were easily the poorest family in our neighborhood. A senator lived in the home to our east. On the west was the shah's tailor. Even the queen's uncle lived in that area. In fact, our street was constantly surveyed by secret-service agents.

Everyone there knew our family could not compete with their wealth. They reacted to that rather rudely. It was as if we didn't belong. We never managed to have one conversation with any of our neighbors.

In the mornings, we used to walk to our school which was in the same neighborhood, but located several blocks away. We brought our own lunch. Our mother used to prepare rice and *khorosht* (a mixture of meat and vegetables). She put the meal into three stackable pots that we had to carry with us each day.

The pots were heavy and awkward to carry. Homa spent a lot of her time complaining about them.

"Why does it bother you so much?" I asked her once.

"Because I feel stupid with these things. We look ridiculous."

"How else would we eat, though?"

"I don't know. It's just that no one else carries pots to school. We shouldn't even be at this school."

"But it's the only school we live near."

"We're too far anyway. The walk takes too long."

"Do you really think so?"

"I just don't like this neighborhood. We don't belong here. Look at the other children; look at their clothes. Our clothes are awful. We're too plain."

I had never considered my sister to be plain before. To me she was the most glamorous person in the world.

She continued, "This place is for the rich. We are scorned every day. I just wish we could leave. Don't you miss the *koocheh*?"

"Not at all. Our new home is much more modern."

"Maybe, but at least we had friends at the other place. Here, we don't know any of the other children because they won't talk to us. We're not rich enough. It's ridiculous!" She became emphatic. "We have money, but not enough to satisfy these people. We weren't born wealthy either."

"We shouldn't think about it."

"Why not! Everybody else does. These people measure the value of everything in their lives by money!"

"You can't be sure of that," I said.

"Sure I can! The other day, I saw one of the girls who lives in the house on the corner. She always wears gorgeous outfits from Paris. Do you know what I had the nerve to do?!"

"What?" I asked.

"I had the nerve to say hello to her. Can you imagine?" The sarcasm in her voice was obvious. "Well! She looked at me with her beady snob-eyes and acted completely shocked by my gesture."

"Why would she—"

"She thought, How dare you try to talk to me with those ugly clothes you wear. Why would you ever?"

I said nothing.

"I just want to go back to the old house. We were the richest family in that neighborhood, but we were nice. We didn't act like these people at all."

She was right about the children in that neighborhood. Most of them went to private schools, so we didn't ever get a chance to really meet them. And at our school, we were the only two students who ate at school with the custodian. The others were picked up by cars and brought home for lunch.

Homa and I got used to playing alone inside the house. We only left when we had to. Homa spent most of her time studying and reading books. Still, life was very peaceful in that house because we were separated from most of the family. We didn't have to worry about fights breaking out between our relatives. Of course, our parents still had their share of disputes.

I still remember the night during the month of Ramadan when Homa was nine and I was seven years old. Our mother was fasting from sunrise to sunset, and she prepared a large dinner that evening. Our father's mother and sister had come over that night to visit. Our mother set a beautiful place setting out on the floor and prepared a four-course dinner for the guests.

Our father came home from work early that night, at sunset. Our grandmother said the appropriate prayers before drinking her tea to break the fast.

The radio started playing theatrical shows throughout the night as we ate. We enjoyed our meal and listened excitedly. We laughed a lot that night. Our moods quickly became jubilant. Our father, however, was not himself. I didn't notice at first.

It was Homa who drew it to my attention. "Brace yourself, Parvin. We're going to be in trouble soon," she whispered.

"What do you mean?"

Our mother was leaning over the place setting, placing a dish of food down. She looked at him briefly and also realized that something was wrong.

She motioned in our direction and looked at his mother. "Did you say something to their father?" Our mother always referred to him as our father. I don't ever remember a time in which she called him her husband. And the practice was mutual. He always called her by her first name.

"No, I didn't say anything," our grandmother responded.

"Then what's wrong with him?" she asked as she looked toward our father.

He stood almost immediately and screamed, "Nothing, I tell you!" He was enraged. Homa and I were frightened. I started crying loudly when he grabbed a dish of rice and threw it out the front window into the yard. He was swearing at our mother as violently as he could.

He threw the china platter and it shattered into pieces. Our mother fled the room.

We followed her and ended up squeezing into the closet to hide with her. I was frantic after having just been dragged around the house by my sister. Homa was upset, too, but she kept control of both of us.

We could hear our father roaming around the house looking for his wife. I knew our mother was in for a beating, but still, I could only cry.

Homa squeezed my fingers and we both clung tightly to our mother. Our father broke through the bedroom door and then tore the closet door from its hinges. He looked like he was ready to kill us.

I screamed hysterically, but Homa put her hand to my chin and held it up so I would keep my attention on her. "Hold on to Mom!" she said.

Our mother lay on the closet floor in a fetal position. I was facing her and my arms were wrapped around her body as far as I could reach.

Homa was shielding her, too, but she had her head turned upward. Our father held his hand high, with his fist clenched.

Homa screamed at him, "Daddy! Stop it! You can't do this to her!"

I don't know why, but something in Homa's voice must have triggered something inside our father. He lowered his fist and stood still, looking toward us. His eyes were angry and his face was tense, but he wasn't moving.

I looked up at them and saw Homa in the doorway of the closet. The two faced each other for a moment that seemed to last forever. And then, our father left the room and the house. He came back sometime late that night. In the morning he was calm. He was normal again and our mother was fine also. The two had many more arguments after that one, but it was the last time he ever tried to hurt his wife.

The episode that summer night only seemed to expand Homa's disdain for our new home. She was ashamed of the violence that existed within our household. It made her feel like the neighbors were correct in thinking we were second-class.

Our other neighbors seemed more civilized. We never heard any of them fight. Homa used to assume that the aggression in our family was a symptom of our relative poverty. To her, poverty made the family ignorant of the civilized way of life, and that ignorance ended up sustaining our low-class appearance.

At about the same time, Homa started picking up an interest in politics. The enormous differences she was discovering between rich and poor inspired her. She initiated a habit of reading. Each day, she would spend a few hours reading history books, newspapers, or anything she could find that seemed interesting.

As she studied, her disdain for the status quo grew. There wasn't much vertical movement in Iran, she found out. People were basically trapped in the economic class they were born to. One of the only exceptions to this came to students who managed to earn a college degree. Homa knew this, and she forced us both to keep studying.

Chapter 6

The Importance of Oil

While we lived in that neighborhood, Homa and I used to go to the Pastor Institute in Tehran to drink the malt they gave out free. It was a rich beverage full of vitamins and minerals. Our mother had us drink it to become stronger.

I was a stubby kid, short and thick. I probably didn't need the extra vitamins. But Homa still had the petite frame with which she was born. On our days off, we would go to the institute, and each of us would drink a pint of the brew.

February 4, 1949, was a Friday. Homa and I were walking home from the institute in the afternoon. We walked slowly. The alcohol made us both feel a little disoriented. The streets were unusually crowded. People hurried around in an unorganized fashion, and Homa and I knew that something was wrong. We couldn't tell what, though.

We walked slowly through the crowds, staring blankly at everyone as they scurried past us. Finally a man came toward us screaming, "The shah's been shot! The shah's been shot!"

The man was disappointed by our reactions. He told us that the king was shot and we barely blinked. He couldn't have known why we were so sedate. It was not common for young girls to walk around with bellies full of beer.

I didn't even know who the shah was, let alone the significance of his being shot. Homa, however, did know what they were talking about and she had a lot to say once she had time to absorb the statements.

"I wonder why anyone would dare to kill the shah?" She said it to me, but I think she was talking to herself.

I responded the same way any younger sister would, by following her lead. "Yeah, Homa, why would anyone want to shoot the shah?"

"I don't know. C'mon, we need to go home and listen to the news on the radio."

The two of us started running through the streets to get home. I'm really surprised we managed to make it home without running into anything or tripping over our feet.

Our house was close to the University of Tehran and the shah's palaces. To get home, we had to run along Kakh Street and pass the four residences where the shah lived.

In our clumsy state, we continued running. We must have made the guards at the palace entrances nervous. They were especially sensitive that day to anyone acting suspiciously. There was a lot of activity around the palaces. Police cars and limousines lined the streets. They were driving in and out of the palace entrances. We noticed that some of the limos would leave one palace's entrance, only to cross the street and enter another one.

We slowed down as we passed the palaces because Homa was curious to find out why everyone seemed so panicked.

We saw a guard who was eyeing us. Homa shouted toward him. "What's going on? What happened to the shah?"

"Nothing. He is fine. You children should go home, quickly." He motioned with his arm to get us to continue walking down the street.

"Who tried to shoot him? What happened?" Homa asked.

He didn't say anything, but continued waving us away.

"But who did it?" She still persisted.

The guard looked at Homa again, and this time he answered. "A man named Naser Fakhr-Araie tried to shoot the shah, but he was shot dead by the security guards. Now really, go home."

We then left and started back toward our street, but other guards were starting to approach us. They were asking us questions about what we were doing so close to the palaces.

Suddenly, the route home seemed unclear. The two of us were lost in a maze of parked cars and guards that covered the streets. I couldn't see the horizon; in each direction my vision was blocked by the sight of jeeps and military trucks. It was frightening because I felt lost. The guards closed in on us. They continued pressuring us with questions.

Homa told them we lived on Moshtagh Street and that we were only trying to return home from the Pastor Institute where we got the brew. The guards didn't believe us. They asked more questions. I was very scared but Homa answered their questions and stayed calm throughout the interrogation.

Eventually, they allowed us to continue on. While we walked away, Homa started explaining something to me.

"They didn't believe us because they don't think we really live around here."

"Why wouldn't they?" I asked.

"We don't look like the kind of people who would live in a neighborhood like this."

At home, Homa sat next to the radio and tried to find out what happened to the shah.

A broadcaster spoke about the attempted assassination and described how Naser Fakhr-Araie shot six bullets toward Shah Mohammad Reza Pahlavi. All but one missed. The shah was hit by a bullet that went through his cheek and came out below his nose, leaving no serious damage.

Homa and I listened to the news while it told the story over and over again until our father came home in the evening. On Fridays, he came home early.

Homa wanted him to explain what had gone on during the day. He was eating the dinner our mother had left for him. Homa sat near him and asked, "Daddy, why did Naser Fakhr-Araie try to shoot the shah?"

"Did you listen to the radio today?" The question surprised him.

"Well, yeah, and everybody outside talks about it, too."

He nodded his head, "You're right about that." Then he lifted a spoon to his mouth and chewed on his food. After a little while he spoke again. "He was probably working for the Tudeh party."

"What is the Tudeh party?" Homa asked.

"Well, the Tudeh party is a group of Iranians who follow Marx and Lenin. They're the Communist party. They want the shah to give the Russians access to the oil in Northern Iran. You see, the British have historically had the right of exploration throughout all of Iran. Some officials want to change that. Some think it would be wise to allow the Russians access to half the nation's oil. The Tudeh party supports this. The shah, however, seems to support the British."

"But how did the British get the rights for the oil in Iran?" asked Homa.

Our father looked at her, and he realized how curious she was becoming. He stopped eating. He pushed his plate away and turned to both of us as if he was going to lecture us like students. He motioned his arms enthusiastically while he spoke. His voice was deep and booming and his enunciation brought life into the words.

"You see, with Iran, it's always going to be about one thing. There are politics of Iran, but the country is governed by the politics of oil. It's deeply rooted in our history.

"In the old times a small fire was started in the southern part of Iran by a man named Zoroaster. The fire raged amazingly and did not burn out. Zoroaster, knowing nothing about petroleum, assumed it to be the act of God. He built a temple around the fire so that people could gather there to pray.

"It wasn't until the latter half of the nineteenth century that two French scientists discovered the source of the fire and found evidence of petroleum deposits on Iranian soil. Soon after the discovery, the scientists found a British venture capitalist named William Knox d'Arcy who was interested in exploring the resource. In 1901 Mozafaredin Shah-e-Ghajar, then king of Iran, entered into a legal agreement with Knox d'Arcy for oil exploration in Iran.

"The agreement gave the British the right of exploration for the petroleum found within the borders of Iran, and its by-products. It was to last for sixty years."

"What does that mean? What is a right of exploration?" Homa asked.

"It gave Knox d'Arcy's company the right to find the oil and natural gas, process them, and sell them to buyers around the world," he explained. "Knox d'Arcy was also permitted to construct pipelines, refineries, and any other companies necessary to properly develop the oil and to sell its products. The agreement also provided that unskilled laborers would be local, but all skilled labor would have to be imported from Britain."

"That doesn't seem fair."

"I think you're right. I also think that has a lot to do with why the Tudeh has grown so much in recent years. A lot of skilled, educated Iranians are looking for a chance to work in a local oil industry. They think the Russians might give them a chance."

"Then it might be good if they get half."

"Well, you can't really say which would be better."

Father was enthusiastic. He loved to talk. He wasn't the kind of person who would talk under any circumstances, however. You had to encourage him. If you came up to him and started asking questions, he would use few words to answer. But if you kept at it long enough, he would realize that you were in the mood to listen. I think that's why he didn't like to talk much with our mother. She was never in the mood to listen. She could only talk.

With our father, though, getting him to talk was a game. If you stayed near him long enough, and asked the right questions, he would open up and flood your mind with information.

Homa asked him for his thoughts about the assassination attempt. Naturally, he had a lot of thoughts on the matter. She tapped into the pool of all that information and he responded. She was a good listener and I was, too. We made an ideal audience.

He continued. "In exchange for the oil, the shah of Iran was to receive 20,000 pounds sterling and 20,000 shares of stock in the company. Also, Knox d'Arcy's company was required to pay 16 percent of their net profits to Iran annually. That was the contract. Later, after World War I British Petroleum bought Knox d'Arcy's company and took over the rights." (The contract was renegotiated in 1932 and in exchange for a larger share of profits, the agreement was to last ninety years instead of sixty. Even then, the Majlis [the Iranian parliament] never ratified the agreement.)

"This year, the issue is back in the Majlis to be ratified. That's probably why the assassination attempt occurred today. The Tudeh party probably found someone to sacrifice and sent him off to kill the shah."

"How many people support this group?"

"A lot, but I think most Iranians would rather not give the right of exploration to any foreign country. They'd rather have that right themselves."

He looked at our faces to see if we were satisfied.

Homa was confused, or at least her expression was. She needed to hear more.

"But Daddy, why is the oil so important?" I asked.

"Oh, sweetheart, it's the source of energy."

Well, if I had known what energy was, I probably would have been able to shed the perplexed look from my face. He knew I was confused.

"Okay, oil provides the energy that runs nearly everything in the world. It's the lifeblood of our planet. Imagine the globe, but think of it as a human body; the oil is like blood. You need it to survive.

"For that reason, countries fight over it. It's in limited supply, you see. There's only a certain amount in the earth and you can only get it in certain places."

"Like here," Homa said.

"Right. There is a lot of oil in Iran, and it's very valuable. It's a source of wealth. I've taken you to the shah's castles, right?"

"Yes," I said.

"They're huge, right? Well, how do you think he pays for it? It's the oil. The oil gives him the castles. It also pays for his army. It gives him the throne, too.

"People can't take the kingdom from the king because no one else can afford an army like his. Some people think the next best thing to taking away his throne is to take the king himself. So they tried to kill him."

"But I don't understand why we have to give the oil to other countries. Why can't we keep it to ourselves?" Homa asked.

"That's a tougher question—"

"Why didn't *we* discover the oil? Why didn't we see the eternal fire as a natural occurrence?!" she persisted.

"Well, we were a different country when the oil was discovered. Nobody in Iran understood what it took to harness all that energy. And now, we've become dependent on the technology of other nations to keep the industry running."

"We could kill the industry, couldn't we? I mean, we could kick all the oil company employees out, right?" Homa asked.

"Well, in theory, yes. But I don't think it would be wise to do so. If we tried to get rid of our oil industry, the rest of the world would probably see to it that we didn't succeed. And besides, we need the money the oil brings in. It's our most valuable resource."

"Why do we need the money so badly?"

"The money allows us to import things from other countries, like fabric, medicine, food, cars, and all sorts of things. It allows us to build schools, railroads, and other badly needed services. It pays to send our top students abroad to learn modern technologies so they can improve the condition of life for all of us."

"But couldn't we stop importing things? Couldn't we just do all those things ourselves?" By this time, my sister was feeling more comfortable with the subject. She was less inquisitive but she started questioning the logic of what she was being told. Surprisingly, to me, she spoke with much enthusiasm. I couldn't understand, at the time, how she could act so interested in such a boring topic. I mean, the two of them were putting me to sleep.

Homa continued. "If we didn't import so much, we wouldn't need the money, right?"

"Sure, but who wants to do that? I like my bike and my house—I couldn't have built this house without using imported goods. It makes life easier."

"But it puts the country in a vulnerable position. If we stopped importing, the rest of the world would leave us alone. In school, they call it imperialism. We should eat only what we can grow within our borders."

"Homa, dear, you have more to learn. It isn't as simple as you make it. Also, you have to remember that we have something the rest of the world needs to survive. If we stop selling them our oil, they'll take it from us. In that way, we're helpless."

"It's all so frustrating," she conceded.

That was the first time I ever saw Homa get excited about politics. After that, she seemed to thrive on the topic. And she was almost always the nationalist. Father tried hard to sway her. He wanted her to understand that leaving the oil in the ground benefited no one.

He felt that "Iranians just can't explore, refine, and market their oil. The British have the know-how, and we have the resource. If our two countries work together we can all benefit from the deal. Isolation brings us nothing."

But Homa heatedly disagreed.

The conversation between Homa and my father continued that night, while I fell asleep next to them on the floor.

That conversation sparked many more of them, and our father always had a desire to teach. From then on, I spent my nights quietly listening to Homa and him discuss the political history of Iran. He taught her how to appreciate the maneuvering that takes place around the world. He taught her how the price of labor in Iran can affect the price of gas in Italy.

I just liked the way he told stories, and I liked the way my sister always asked questions. Most of the time, I fell asleep halfway through their talks. Still, after listening to them for just a few months, I think I knew enough about Iranian history to cover my twelve years of education in school.

After the assassination attempt, the shah became more active in the country's political affairs. In order to promote support for his regime, he traveled a lot inside and outside of the country. Each time he returned to Tehran, his motorcade would travel through parts of the city and to his palaces. Children that went to schools close to the route were taken out of class so they could line the street and wave flags or applaud as the motorcade went by. Often, the event would leave hundreds of children waiting in the streets for hours.

On one occasion, I was very ill, but had gone to school anyway. Upon arrival in the morning, we were told about the shah's return from a recent trip. We were going to be walked to the motorcade route.

It was raining heavily that morning, and Homa was worried about my health. After we made it to the main street, she tried to keep me from having to stay.

She approached the schoolmistress and pleaded with her. "My sister has a very bad cold, and she will only get worse if she waits out here in the rain for the next few hours. Please excuse us, and I will take her home."

"I can't do that," she said. "All of you are expected to be here. If I excused the two of you, what would everyone else say? I'd have to excuse them, too. Anyway, she came to school on her own, didn't she?"

"But she didn't think she'd be standing in the rain all day!" Homa was upset, but she wasn't changing the schoolmistress's mind.

We were listening to a radio in the distance to determine when the shah would be passing by. We heard the announcer excitedly describing the king's arrival in light of the weather: "Today, the shah is coming home and the sky is shedding tears of joy and happiness."

Homa looked at our schoolmistress. "The last time we did this, the sun was shining and the radio announcer said the skies are glowing with joy and happiness." She acted disgusted.

"And when it once snowed on the day of his arrival they said, 'Today the shah is coming home and the sky has wrapped the earth in white sheets, like a bride prepared for her groom.' So what other weather could there be? It's just ridiculous!"

Still, the schoolmistress did not budge. We both had to stay there in the rain most of the day. The bad weather delayed the shah's arrival.

Homa was bitter for the rest of the day. She kept telling me, "Everything in this country is done by force. We're never given a choice about things. In this kingdom, we're only subjects, and subjects have no rights at all."

She continued, "A society should protect its children, and not force them to stand in rain and snow to greet a person they don't even know."

By the time we got home, Homa and I were completely soaked. I ended up with an awful case of bronchitis that left me bedridden for four months. Homa never stopped complaining about the ritual which she blamed for my illness.

In fact, as my life went on my colds were always followed by slight cases of bronchitis. Any time I asked my sister for help, she spent a little of her time grumbling about the system that caused my chronic health problem.

We moved out of the house on Moshtagh Street when Homa completed the fifth grade. We had to rent an apartment for six months until our house in the *koocheh* became vacant and we could move back into it.

At the apartment, we had a neighbor named Nadjista Khanoum. She worked as a maid for her sister. At that time, she was in her late forties. She was an attractive woman with a pleasant personality. Homa and I could never understand why she worked as her sister's maid.

One day the two of us were playing in our yard when we saw Nadjista working in her front yard. She had spread a lot of vegetables on a piece of cloth and was cleaning them for dinner. Homa saw her there and she walked over. I came with her.

"Nadjista, why do you work for your sister? I mean, why don't you have your own home and your own family?" she asked.

"Do you like what you do?" I interrupted. "I mean, are you happy?"

Nadjista let out a deep sigh and looked at both of us. She must have been embarrassed by our questions, but we were too young to know better. She smiled slightly and continued working on the vegetables while she spoke. "Well, girls, I can't say that I'm unhappy. But I don't really like living my life as a maid either," she said.

"Then, why do you?" Homa asked.

"I don't really have a choice. It's just the way things have worked out."

"What do you mean?" Homa persisted.

"When I was fourteen, my parents married me to a man who was already married."

"Really?" My sister and I were shocked because we never knew it was permitted.

"He was also thirty years older than I was, and if that wasn't enough, he was fat and ugly."

"Oh, gosh!" I said, "what did you do?"

"I refused to accept him. I refused to live with him, and I refused to sleep with him." Then she stopped working on the vegetables and looked toward the front door for a moment. "He decided to punish me. He told me he wouldn't divorce me till my hair became the color of my teeth. It's all I have now, to be a maid. You see, I am still his wife."

She went back to her vegetables for a while and Homa and I just watched her. We were silent. Then she spoke again.

"I am still his wife, and he has refused to divorce me. Whatever I've wanted to do has been impossible. I need his permission to go to school. I need his permission to get a job. Of course, I need it to leave the country, too. He just won't give it to me."

She took a deep breath and continued. "My life ended when I was only fourteen. Now, I'm forty-eight. I have nothing. I have no education, no skills, and my father and brother are dead. I have to work for my sister so my brother-in-law won't feel burdened by having to support me."

Homa and I were amazed by the story. Neither of us could understand why something so sad could be allowed. We asked her to explain.

"Well, in our religion a man is permitted to have four permanent wives at one time and as many temporary wives as he wishes. A woman, of course, must stay loyal to one husband. It is even said in the Koran that women are the grazing fields of men."

"But," Homa asked, "what's the difference between permanent and temporary wives?"

Nadjista explained, "In our religion a marriage is an agreement between a man and a woman to stay together for an established period of time. When the time is up, the marriage is annulled.

"A permanent marriage is an agreement for ninety-nine years because people can't live that long, and a temporary one is arranged for any period."

"Any period?" Homa asked.

"A couple can be married for ten minutes, or a year, any period. In a permanent marriage a *mullah* performs the ceremony and the event is registered with the state and on each person's birth certificate."

"What about temporary marriages?" I asked.

"Those are performed by the man and are not registered at all. The man usually asks a woman if she would become his wife for an hour in exchange for forty or fifty rials. If the woman says yes, then they are married, and when the hour is up so is the marriage."

"How many men do this?"

"The problem is, if the woman gets pregnant, she has no way of proving who the father is. The religion tells them to let one hundred days pass between encounters with different men. But even then, there's no legal document to demonstrate the temporary marriage."

She continued, "Then, if the woman gets pregnant and cannot find the father, she has to do something with the baby."

"What can she do?" Homa asked.

"If she can afford it, she can raise the child herself. Usually, though, she has to give it up to an orphanage and let others care for it. Most orphans are products of temporary marriages."

Nadjista stopped talking and continued preparing the food. Homa and I sat with her and tried to help a little. Then Homa was curious again.

"What happened to the man you were forced to marry?"

"Oh, nothing. He married again. He's now living with three wives that keep separate rooms in the same house. He has children from each one of them. I guess his life is fine," she said.

"Does he pay for your support?" asked Homa.

"No. Not at all."

"Isn't he supposed to?" Homa persisted.

"Not if I refuse to live with him. In our religion, a woman must be prepared to meet her husband's demands unconditionally. If she doesn't do that, he has the right to deny her even the most basic needs."

"It's so sad," Homa said softly.

"Yeah, it's sad," I said.

The two of us thanked Nadjista and walked back home.

"It has to change. We have to change this system," Homa said this to me in a deep, authoritative voice.

That night, I couldn't sleep because I was thinking about the conversation we had with Nadjista. I wondered if Homa felt the same way.

"Homa, are you awake?" I asked.

"Yeah, why?"

"I was just thinking about Nadjista Khanoum."

"She's had an awful life," Homa admitted.

"I know. Isn't it scary? I don't think I ever want to get married."

"Neither do I."

"What happens if somebody makes us marry some old guy when we're too young? Homa, you're already eleven. In two years you'll be the age Mommy was when she got married. Doesn't that scare you?"

"I don't think Daddy would allow it. He wants us to study and become professionals. We just have to work hard and do well in school. Let's sleep and be ready for class tomorrow. Good night, Parvin."

"Yeah, good night."

Chapter 7

The Eagle and the Raven

While we lived in the apartment, we used to gather at night by the radio after we ate. On Fridays we used to listen to a radio program hosted by Houshang Mostoufi.

Mostoufi was well known in Iran. He used his show to recite short stories and poems. His voice was unique; he could read things in a beautiful manner.

We were most touched by a poem he read called "The Eagle." Roughly translated, the poem was as follows:

An eagle was flying high above the mountains when he saw a raven well below him. He rememberd that ravens always live longer than eagles and so he flew down toward the raven to ask him what the secret to his longevity was.

The raven told the eagle that the secret was two-fold. "It is my low flying, and my diet."

"I can fly low also," said the eagle. "But I feed off of birds I catch in flight."

"And that is the problem. You must learn to eat as I do. Come with me to the swamp tomorrow, and I will show you how."

The next morning the eagle went to the swamp with the raven and watched the raven feasting on the rubbish in the swamp. He watched the raven pull apart the decomposed carcasses and sift his beak through the mud.

And to this, the eagle decided, "My friend, the raven, I can fly low, for the rest of my short life, but there is no way I can feed on this scum that gathers on the swamp floor."

The raven looked up to respond to the eagle, but all there was in the sky was the small silhouette of the eagle flying high above.

Homa and I were excited by the words of the poem. We asked each other which life we would prefer, that of the eagle or the raven. Homa said she wanted to live like the eagle. She preferred a short, challenging life garnished with the power and freedom to do whatever she wanted.

Later that year, Homa wrote a composition of her own for school. She called it "Who Is Happy?"

What is happiness? Who is happy? Perhaps no one. It could be that happiness is just a myth—a fragment of man's imagination. I know of no person who could be called fortunate, or happy. Look at these people:

A person studies hard to become a doctor, or perhaps a lawyer. The person marries, has children, and becomes a symbol of success to everyone. Then all of a sudden his child is diagnosed with leukemia and he spends the rest of his life in mourning.

Or a young couple meet and fall in love. They find happiness in each other, and before they're old enough to appreciate it, one dies. The other is left to mourn.

When all these disasters can pop up in our lives at any time, why do we speak of happiness?

People talked about that composition for weeks. Whenever there were guests, our mother would have Homa read it for them. I never grew tired of hearing it.

Homa's ability to write improved dramatically while she was in the sixth grade. But what surprised me was the way in which she began to express herself in public. I'm not sure who brought it out of her, but Homa's first public protest occurred at about the same time.

Our cousin Nahid was still living in the *koocheh*, and we still spent a lot of time with her. By now, she'd become the top student in her second-grade class, but her school wouldn't have it. They wanted to rank her second so that another girl, the daughter of a powerful man, could enjoy the honor.

At the assembly, the principal made the announcement, introducing Nahid as the second-best student in her class. Of course Homa knew this was going to happen, so when it did she stood up in the audience and confronted the people onstage. She asked Nahid to read her grade-point average aloud.

She did and then Homa turned to the other girl, who refused to answer. Then Homa asked the principal to read it. She wouldn't either.

The young girl was crying and the principal was trying to deal with her. She didn't see Homa approach the stage, take both report cards, and read them to the audience.

The young girl fled the room quickly, taking the principal with her. They were humiliated.

The Arrival of Mossadegh

During those years, political topics attracted more attention from the people of Tehran than it ever had before. The country was starting to show signs of deterioration. The shah, who was still feverishly trying to promote his political stance, was having trouble finding a prime minister who would be a powerful leader for the country but who would not threaten his own stature as the king. He was replacing prime ministers rapidly as the political climate oscillated, and a few of them were even assassinated. It was a turbulent time.

The government was coming down heavily on the media to prevent them from publishing criticism of the regime. Newspapers were banned and reporters were executed for committing what were labeled as antigovernment crimes.

Although outlawed in 1949, the Tudeh party was flourishing, and most young people were getting actively involved in politics at some level. There was unrest everywhere and demonstrations were being held daily. Truckloads of Tudeh party members chanted slogans and drove from one side of Tehran to the other. We used to watch them as we came home from school.

And then, in 1951, Dr. Mohammad Mossadegh assumed the position of prime minister of Iran. During his reign, Iran became a different country. He took power with the specific intention of nationalizing the oil industry. He did so during the first year of his reign, and formed the Iranian National Oil Company. The act, however, was not well received by the international community. They recognized the tremendous value of what they had lost.

Homa and I tried to pay attention to the events of those days. We were overwhelmed by the changes, though.

Indeed, many Iranians were enthusiastic about the moves Mossadegh made during his first year. Seeing the British leave Iran brought satisfaction to many people as they rallied in nationalism. Many weren't so convinced, however. Our father, for one, was skeptical. He feared that Iran would suffer once the foreign technicians that maintained the oil company were sent home.

Mossadegh quickly became a very popular leader. No one, therefore, was prepared when he gave his resignation to the shah on July 17, 1952. And once the shah named Ghavam-Saltaneh as the new Prime Minister, the people of Iran knew what was happening.

Ghavam-Saltaneh was an old man with very weak leadership skills. He appeared to be little more than a puppet for the shah. The people realized that the leader they supported had been stolen from them. They reacted with violence.

July 21, 1952

Our Aunt Maryam was a nurse and had just finished her work at the hospital. The road to her home was blocked by demonstrations. She came to our house instead.

"There are hundreds of dead bodies in the hospital. We don't know what to do with them. People's limbs are lying in the hallways. All you can hear are the cries of men, young and old," she reported as she walked through the front door.

"Is it that bad?" asked Homa.

"I've never seen anything like it," she replied.

"I wish all of this would stop," said Homa.

Earlier in the week, Homa and I had gone shopping and seen thousands of men and women marching through the center of town, toward the shah's palaces. They were being stopped by the military as they approached the streets around his residence.

The crowds were shouting the same slogan in unison: "Death to the shah! Death or Mossadegh!"

Tehran was in chaos. The city looked like a war zone. We were grateful that it was summer and we didn't have to go to school through the turmoil.

Homa asked Maryam about what she saw that day. "What did you see coming over?"

"Riots. It looked like several riots were going on. People want Mossadegh back. The Ayatollah Kashani has issued a *fetwa*, a religious call, asking for people to resist the dictatorial orders of Ghavam-Saltaneh, and the people have responded by protesting. There are tanks and soldiers all over the city."

We stayed next to the radio that day and listened as the riots continued outside. Our father came home and explained more of the details of the strife. He said that many of the political and religious parties had united to bring Mossadegh back.

"People say that since Ghavam-Saltaneh is too old, they are suspicious of the motives in giving him the position," he said.

About five hundred people died during the protest. Most of them were young men. Still, by 8 P.M., the shah finally gave in and reappointed Dr. Mossadegh only four days after his resignation.

Our father asked us to come with him and our Uncle Hossain to a gathering in front of Mossadegh's home. There was a huge crowd when we got there, so Uncle Hossain put me on his shoulders to see better.

I was amazed. I'd never seen that many people in one place before. The crowd was vast. Mossadegh renewed the feeling of national pride in Iran by demonstrating that he could stand up to Britain, a global superpower. That night, we watched him greet the audience from the balcony of his bedroom. Homa and I were impressed by Mossadegh. He seemed to be a tremendous leader.

The Holy City of Mashed One Year Later

A year passed and political pressures mounted in Tehran. Tension grew within factions of the government and Homa struggled to comprehend the issues. Our father could see that she wanted to understand the current events, and he wanted to help her. For that reason, he brought us all to the city of Mashed.

Mashed is a sacred place for Shiite Moslems. It is rich with history, and many prominent Iranians have been buried there. Our father was an ideal tour guide. He loved to tell us the history of Iran and show us the places where that history took place. We knew that if he had been able to attend school, he would have been a historian.

We stayed in the city of Mashed the first two days and visited the shrine of Imam Reza. On the morning of the first day, we heard that the shah and his wife, Soraya, were leaving Iran for good. The news didn't phase us. We spent the afternoon touring the shrine.

That day, Homa and I were harassed by several *mullahs*. We'd never worn *chadors* (the body veil required for women in Shiite Moslem countries) before and we couldn't keep them from slipping back and exposing our heads. Every time a *mullah* passed by us, we were slapped on the forehead. It was their way of explaining what we'd been doing wrong.

The two of us got so frustrated that we ended up lashing out at one of the *mullahs*. He was walking toward us while we were outside and we could see his hand reaching toward Homa's face. She kicked him in the shin before he could slap her. While he bent over to rub the sting from his shin, we laughed at the sound of his profane cursing.

The shrine was an unforgettable sight for both of us. It is a gorgeous structure that was rebuilt in the fifteenth century around the tomb of Imam Reza, who was killed in a religious battle during the Arab occupation of Iran in 817 C.E.

People believe that a wish made the first time they see the shrine will be granted.

When we were there, Shiite Moslems had come from all over the world to worship. Some came barefoot, with torn clothing and sacks filled with money to give the imam. Thousands were shoving each other to get close to the metal bars surrounding the tomb. Once there, they tossed handfuls of money onto the grave. Then, they would grab one of the bars with one hand while their bodies floundered helplessly with the pressure of the crowd. They would beat themselves with their free hand and cry to the imam until they lost consciousness.

On our second day in Mashed, we returned to the shrine. Our parents left us at its entrance, and Homa and I watched as hoards of people came to complete their pilgrimages.

One woman arrived holding an infant with her right arm with three other children trying to hold her free arm. The baby looked malnourished. It was clinging to its mother's thin breast, trying to feed on whatever milk was there.

All of these pilgrims were barefooted. They had come miles across the desert. The woman was one among many.

"Homa?" I asked. "How can people be this way?"

"I don't know."

"I've never seen anything like it."

"I know." Homa and I were sitting on the steps that led to the shrine. She was watching the line of people approaching us from the distance. The crowds of people made a long human trail on the landscape.

"Look at them," she said. "They have nothing. They could be starving, and they come here to give money to the imam, a man who died centuries ago."

When our parents came back, we went to visit the Imam Reza Museum. We were mesmerized by the sight of the incredible wealth displayed. There were huge carpets, beautiful jewels, pure gold sculptures, and magnificent paintings covering the walls.

It was Homa who spoke first. "I wonder what all of this is worth. How many people could be fed if they sold just one sculpture?"

"You should have seen the wealth around the imam's grave." Our father had a smirk on his face. "They need giant shovels to clean it out at night."

"You would think they would use some of it to clothe the people lying on the streets," Homa commented.

I knew the trip to the shrine had a tremendous effect on my sister, but I was glad this part of our trip was ending.

The Coup

The next day, August 19, 1953, we left Mashed in the morning for Tus, the city where Ferdosi was buried. His tomb was in the center of a garden decorated with his poetry.

Together, we had a nice lunch in a small restaurant that bordered the park. Afterward, we walked through the garden and listened while our father recited another story from the *Shahnameh.*

It was a short bus trip from Tus back to Mashed, but it was interrupted by a gang of young men blocking the road. They were rioters, and they appeared to have looted a shoe store and a liquor store because they were very drunk and had draped themselves with new shoes.

This crowd was chanting, "Long live the shah! Death to Mossadegh!" It had taken a year for hordes of rioters in Iran to completely reverse their allegiance.

The driver pleaded with the crowd to make them leave, but they were too drunk to listen. We closed all of our windows and the bus crept slowly forward so that the force of the vehicle would push us through the crowds outside.

It was a frightening experience. Homa and I worried that the vehicle would turn over from the weight of the men hanging on its sides.

We finally arrived at the terminal in Mashed and went straight to the house where we were staying. The radio was on and several people were gathered around it. They were listening to the British Broadcasting Corporation.

"General Zahedi and the Iranian forces have completed a successful coup in Tehran, and all government agencies are under their control. The city is in chaos. Mossadegh is missing. General Zahedi has become the new prime minister by the order of the shah."

We all sat quietly and listened to the report. After a while I looked at my sister and found her weeping.

"Why are you crying?" I asked.

"I'm worried."

"About the family?"

"About everything. I hate all these killings. We have to go back."

"Why?" I asked.

She turned to our father. "Daddy, we have to go back."

"We should," he agreed. "We need to check on Uncle Hossain, my sisters, and the rest of the family."

Homa and I couldn't understand why the people in Iran had changed their position so quickly. Our father told us he believed a foreign power must have been involved. Years later, we learned of the CIA operation organized to topple Mossadegh in 1953. With his departure, so too departed Iran's hopes to free the oil industry from foreign control.

A consortium was formed between the eight largest oil companies in the world. The consortium assumed power as a contracting agent for the operation of the oil fields and the sale of their end product.

Chapter 8

Nothing for Decent Girls

By the time of the coup, we were living in the *koocheh* again. The *koocheh* seemed the same, except that Homa and I were now a few years older. However, several changes occurred in our family. For one, it was the first time Homa and I ever had to attend school separately. Also, our mother reestablished a friendship with a religious woman named Mrs. Kobra. Mrs. Kobra ran a religious day care for preschool children.

Our mother started abiding by the rules of *hijab*, the Islamic dress code for women set forth in the Koran. Under these rules, women are required to cover their bodies from head to toe.

Our mother started wearing long, heavy black stockings; long-sleeved shirts; a skirt; and a shawl that concealed her hair. All of her clothes were black, and she covered them with a long sheet called the *chador* which was also black.

Homa and I couldn't understand what caused our mother to undergo such a lifestyle change. We hated it. Seeing her in black every day was depressing.

Homa constantly questioned our mother about her apparent religious revival. Still, the woman seemed to enjoy her new life. She started studying the Koran with several other women her age, spending much of her time with them.

Father had a life of his own also. He went to work in the morning and came back very late at night. He no longer read to us because we were old enough now to read to ourselves.

Homa and I kept busy with our schoolwork. It was odd. We were less of a united family than ever. Even on Fridays, our day off, when we wanted to see a movie, we did that separately.

For the next few years, Homa and I occupied ourselves with school and our mother became lethargic and depressed. We did not understand why, but she started spending days lying in bed with a hot-water bottle until her friends or relatives would come around to keep her company.

Eventually, Homa convinced our mother to shed her traditional outfit. She did this by constantly preaching to her about the rights of women and the concept of equality. These were things she was learning in high school.

In 1955 we left the *koocheh* for good and moved to a much nicer neighborhood close to the University of Tehran.

In that neighborhood, we both decided it was time for us to learn how to ride bicycles. We approached our father about it, but he refused to let us.

"What's wrong with a girl riding a bicycle?!" I demanded. "What are we supposed to do?! Boys can ride bicycles and horses! They can go swimming. They can play tennis! What can we do? We want to enjoy life too!"

Homa was also raving. "I hate this place! How can we live in a country that forces us to be people we're not? We'd like to live the way boys do. They have it better!" She was fifteen at the time and was furious with our father.

"A decent girl does not ride a bicycle!" he insisted.

"What does a decent girl do, then? Should she point her body toward Mecca and just die?" Homa asked.

Homa gave up. I cried for a little while before I gave up and then found Homa in our room.

"Parvin," she said, "don't worry. We'll get a bicycle, and then we'll learn to ride it."

"How?" I asked.

"I'll tell you tomorrow when we go to school," she replied.

"Why can't you tell me now?"

"Just wait until tomorrow."

The next day, I was eager to find out what Homa had to say. As usual, I got ready to leave for school first. It always took Homa forever to get ready in the morning. She had to comb her hair several times and change the outfit under her uniform at least twice. At this time she was even applying a little eye makeup.

We finally managed to leave the house; and as soon as we started walking, I asked Homa how she thought we could get a bicycle.

"If we talk to our physical education teacher, and then get every girl in our school to pay ten rials, we can buy one bike for everyone to share. Our teacher is young and modern and it's an all-girl school, so it should be easy to ride there."

"Wow, Homa. That's a great idea! We can use our allowance for it." At the time, we got five rials per day to spend on whatever we liked. This was just two days' allowance and not a big sacrifice.

It took us a week to raise enough money for a bike. It was probably the first bicycle ever used in an all-girls school in Iran. We learned to ride it after one lunch period. However, the learning experience left us badly bruised, and the bike requiring a trip to the repair shop.

Once we learned to ride, it was difficult for our father to stop us from doing so outside of school.

"Homa, let's go rent some bikes and go for a ride," I suggested one Friday.

"I don't think they'll rent one to us," said Homa. "I mean, because we're girls."

"They won't care," I insisted. "They say if you pay enough, you can even play with the king's mustache. People can't say no to money. Let's try."

We spent that afternoon riding bikes around our neighborhood. We had a ball, but our father wanted to kill us afterward.

He gave us another lecture on how to be decent and respectable girls.

"What's so disrespectful about riding a bike?" Homa asked him.

"Nice girls don't ride bikes," he responded.

"Why not?!" she asked.

"Well, look around you!" He was getting frustrated. "Does your mother ride a bike? Do your aunts? Do the girls in the neighborhood ride bikes? Why do you two have to? Why do you want to ruin my reputation?"

"Why should it ruin your reputation? You ride a bike to work every day, and no one cares!"

"It's different," he responded.

Our father was never able to argue with Homa and me at the same time. It worked against him. He had no chance especially since he could never get any help from his wife. She never got involved in our fights with him.

Most of the time we recognized when he didn't have good answers to our questions. He may even have been asking himself the same question, *Why can't girls ride bikes?*

We fought for hours before he compromised. "Why don't you both go to your Aunt Pari's house when you want to ride bikes. You can do it in their neighborhood. That way I don't have to be humiliated in front of my colleagues by my daughters on their day off."

We agreed and from then on we spent a lot of our Fridays at our Aunt Pari's. In her neighborhood, we could rent bikes with our cousins and enjoy our days off.

High school went very well for Homa and me. We were both good students and we took care of each other. However, our experiences were slightly different. I focused most of my energy on expanding my understanding of mathematics. Homa studied science and politics. She used to debate students and teachers about current politics. She was fascinated by the arena.

Another reason our experiences were different had to do with boys. As I got older, I kept my solid frame. I always looked fairly average in a crowd of girls. Homa, however, grew to be incredibly graceful and delicate. By the time she turned sixteen, she had the face of Sophia Loren. Her frame was still slight, and this made her stand out as a gorgeous, fragile woman.

Because of her beauty, and because of her academic abilities, Homa was highly desired by the males in our community. Dating, however, was prohibited in Iran when we were young, as it still is today. When young men wanted to show their affection for my sister, all they could do was to follow her around and write letters to her, and hope they weren't caught.

Making sure the letters were delivered was the toughest challenge. They had to pass them any way they could. Sometimes they would wrap the letters around small rocks and toss them through our open window into our room. Other times, they would walk past us on the street and drop the notes into our bags.

When Homa was sixteen, there was one particularly persistent suitor. He was probably nineteen years old, tall, and had blond hair. We had a large glass window protected by decorated steel bars in our bedroom. It faced the street in front of the house. This boy used to stand outside the house and wait for Homa to leave so he could follow her wherever she went.

One afternoon, Homa and I were in our room, lying on our stomachs on the bed. We were peering through the drapes, staring at the young man who was waiting for Homa. He was sitting across the street and leaned up against the wall of someone else's home.

We knew that if Homa tried to leave the house that day, the young man would follow her through the streets. He always did. Homa used to get frustrated by him. She did not like the idea of being followed. She thought of the young man as a stalker.

In our room, we had a large oak wardrobe that leaned against the wall opposite the window. While we stared at the boy, I could see the reflection of this wardrobe in the window. Its doors were wide open and there were two coats hanging inside. These were made for us by a tailor that our mother knew. They were the same color and were made from the same fabric. The styles were different though. Mine had a strait back and Homa's was tied with a belt at the waist.

Homa and I were both looking at the boy and thinking of the coats. We got up and walked to the wardrobe. Homa reached for her coat. Then she draped her coat around me and buttoned it from the bottom.

Her hands worked smoothly and quickly over the buttons. They were delicate and graceful, like the rest of her. When she fastened the top button, I felt the pinch of the collar lightly grip my neck. Homa's hands had fallen to my waist where she was tying the belt.

"Now you are ready," she said. "I want you to go outside and walk toward Shah-Reza Avenue as if you were going to take the bus somewhere. You'll take the boy with you and then I'll walk the other way after he leaves."

I left the house and he followed me, just as she said he would. While I walked down the street, I heard his footsteps behind me. I was nervous because I thought he might figure out what we had done. But he did not. He followed me for several blocks. Once I reached Shah-Reza Avenue, I turned toward him to let him know.

We did this to the boy a lot. I always paid close attention to the look on his face when I finally turned around. He had a frustrated, angry look every time.

Chapter 9

Medical School

High school ended in 1958 for Homa. She was the top student in her graduating class. She had no time to celebrate, however, because she'd decided to apply for medical school.

She spent that summer preparing for her entrance examinations to the University of Tehran. It was the finest university in Iran, but getting an opportunity to study there was very difficult. The admissions department was flooded with applications from qualified students graduating from high schools around the country. The fact that it was a public school with free tuition made it a feasible option for many prospective students.

The year Homa applied at the medical school, she was competing with thousands of other students. They all had to take a comprehensive examination in Tehran, in August, and only three hundred of them could be offered admission.

Homa knew it was imperative that she do well on the exam, so she maintained a rigorous preparation schedule. At first, she studied with several students her age. I remember some of them because they used to gather at our house. When they took breaks, they would have snacks with the family. Eventually, though, she stopped studying in groups and started working with a young man named Mohsen every day.

People were surprised to see Homa working so often with a boy. It was fairly unusual in Iran for men and women to study together. Still, for two months both of them followed a brutal schedule, studying every day and every night, taking breaks only to eat.

Mohsen's presence in our house was bothersome at times because he wasn't very friendly. He didn't socialize at all, and Homa didn't spend much time with the family anymore.

It was a relief for all of us when the day finally came, and Homa took her test. She came home after the exam and went straight to bed. The next morning, she was tense. She worried about whether her performance was good enough to get her into medical school.

I will never forget how difficult it was for us to wait for those results. For weeks, Homa couldn't sit still. She was constantly nervous and her voice always shook when she spoke. At times, she would sit in our house and adjust her posture constantly and her hands would pick at each other whenever they came together. I remember it vividly now, because she looked the same way toward the end of her life.

Every evening Homa and I walked to the store on the corner of our street and bought a newspaper, hoping that the exam's results would be printed that day. On the night they were, we read them in the street before we walked back home.

Homa's study-partner, Mohsen, was easy to find. He was one of the first ten names mentioned. The list was published in order of the scores. When we followed the trail of names down Homa began doubting herself. She kept saying, "I knew it. I knew I didn't make it."

I didn't say anything. I was running down the list, reading every name and searching for our last name. On the second page, she was listed as number 237. I let out a scream and we burst into laughter when we saw the name, Homa Darabi. We ran toward our house.

At the entrance to the house, I called to our mother.

"Homa is going to be a doctor!"

"She was accepted?!" Our mother came out of her room and joined us. The three of us celebrated in the middle of our hallway. We stayed there together, and enjoying the feeling for a long time.

Our mother never had the opportunity in her life to be anything but our father's wife, and now she was looking into the eyes of her daughter and dreaming about what she was going to become. She started crying in a most unfamiliar way. I didn't understand it then, but I can recognize it now as I remember that day.

The news of Homa's acceptance lifted the entire family to a new level. She was the first person in our family to pass the entrance examinations to the University of Tehran's School of Medicine. It elevated us to a new social class. We developed a self-pride that common people aren't supposed to enjoy.

For weeks, it was all my mother would talk about. Her daughter becoming a doctor of medicine. In Iran, it is one of the greatest honors a parent can enjoy.

We had another cousin, Saeed, who once applied to the medical school. He wasn't as lucky, though. After he failed to score in the top three hundred of his applicant pool, he was sent to Germany to study.

A few years before Homa received her good news, I remember our family went to the Mehrabad Airport to see him off. Homa and I were young children. It was the first time we'd ever been inside an airport. We spent most of the time staring out the windows of the airport watching crew members work on the aircraft outside. Before, we had only seen planes in the air flying over the city. In the air, they looked small and insignificant. At night they looked like moving stars. My sister and I were amazed by the size of the planes. They were huge. Homa told me she never thought the planes would be so big and carry so many people.

As his departure time approached, Saeed said good-bye to everyone and went through customs. Our family went outside to the fenced-off area where we could watch the planes take off. After about two hours, we saw Saeed leave the customs area and walk to the plane that was taking him to Germany. He quickly climbed the staircase to the plane. When he reached the last stair, he turned and waved to all of us. It was an uplifting moment. We all waved back and screamed at him while he boarded.

I was so excited that I turned to Homa and said, "One day, Homa, I will wave to you from that step. I will leave this place and go far away. I'll find someplace where being female won't be a handicap."

"Where will you find such a place? I don't know where one exists," she answered.

"America. What about America?"

"There is trouble there too. You will be a woman wherever you go."

"I don't care, there must be a place. I have all my life to find it."

The educational system of Iran considered Saeed a failure because he never passed their university's entrance examinations. But he completed medical school in Germany and became a prominent doctor and professor of medicine there. He still practices in the city of Essen. Although he visits Iran periodically, he never returned for good.

What seemed to be an impossible dream for me at the time came true ten years later when I climbed the steps of an airplane and left Iran aboard an Air France carrier on February 7, 1964. Like Saeed, I never went back to stay. Today, most of our extended family is scattered around the world. Almost all of us have become accomplished individuals, adopted by our new countries. Yet we all still long for the home we once knew and the experience we enjoyed of being a family. Our children grow up alone, without the love of their grandparents and extended families.

A few days into medical school, Homa came home from class with a small box. I found her in our room staring inside the box which was on the floor.

"What are you doing?" I asked.

"I brought this frog from the university. I have to remove its digestive track." She continued looking at the frog.

"Really," I said. "What are you waiting for?"

"I'd have to kill the frog," she explained.

"Of course you would. What's wrong with that?"

"You know I don't like to kill things!"

"But, Homa, you're going to be a doctor one day. You'll have to get used to seeing living things die. You know that, don't you?"

"I know, but it's hard."

"Well, you have to do it. I'll stay with you and help."

She started by giving the frog some chloroform to knock it out.

Next, she laid it on its back and marked where she would cut. She was slow and meticulous with each of her movements. When she raised her surgical knife and pierced the frog's belly, the frog reacted and leapt away from her hands.

I followed the frog's flight onto the floor with my eyes in order to keep it from getting away. But when I caught it and turned around, Homa was lying on the floor. She had fainted.

I poured some cold water on her face and she was revived. She started again, using a little more chloroform before cutting. Once she started, she seemed to forget how hesitant she had been, and she worked very quickly.

Within a few months, I would stop by the anatomy lab at the university to walk home with her, and she would be working on human corpses. It was amazing how quickly Homa became desensitized to blood. It was hard to believe that this woman who fainted when she cut into a small frog was now removing body parts without an instant of hesitation.

When Homa began attending medical school, I thought she would stop paying so much attention to politics. I was wrong. Studying at the university only fueled her desire to learn more about current issues.

Homa became an active member of the Pan-Iranist party, headed by Dariush-e-Frouhar in 1958, after she began medical school. It was a nationalist party that supported a pro-Mossadegh philosophy.

I was also a member for a short time. Homa recruited me and I went to a few meetings. The party had a language of its own. There was a secret salute, a weekly meeting, and an underground newsletter they circulated regularly.

Over time, Homa got more involved in political activism. She had a natural affinity for the subject. I think it may have been a way to escape the pressures of her schooling.

Her obsession was fueled by the fact that domestic politics were more volatile than ever. Student protests on the university campus during the early sixties were the norm. And each time there was a protest, a handful of students would be rounded up and punished. Still, the violent countermeasures only seemed to drive the students to protest more. At the time, the shah was purchasing arms from foreign governments to combat domestic opposition to his monarchy.

Homa was an active part of many of these demonstrations. While I was still in high school, I walked past the university on my way home to look for Homa. I wanted to see if she was out on the grounds passing out literature or holding sit-ins. Several times, I would see her on a platform stage, addressing the audience. She would plead with them to fight for freedom, democracy, and human rights. It was an amazing source of pride to see my sister up there addressing hundreds of people. Her passion was inspiring. It seemed to ignite from a fire within her.

Watching her was a dangerous act, however. When the police came, they arrested everyone. It didn't matter that I was an innocent bystander. I was arrested twice and taken to the Savak (the secret police) offices for questioning.

Interestingly, the offices were located inside ordinary homes in residential neighborhoods. Each time, bystanders like myself were taken from the university grounds and subjected to intense questioning. It was a scare tactic. Over time, this process only made us more adept at answering questions quickly and thinking on our feet.

Chapter 10

In the Tentacles of the Savak

On a January afternoon in 1961, Homa and I were at home alone. The university had been shut down for the week due to several successive antigovernment demonstrations. The unrest was a result of the parliament having been dissolved without the commencement of new elections.

We were in our room and Homa was napping when I heard the doorbell ring. I went to the door and found Parvaneh, the wife of Dariush-e-Frouhar. Parvaneh was our father's second cousin.

I greeted her. "I'm surprised to see you. What brings you over?"

"Is Homa home?" she asked quickly.

"Of course," I replied. "Please come in."

"No, I want to know if Homa's here." She looked nervous and wouldn't come in.

"I'm here, Parvaneh." Homa was standing on the stairs facing the front door. She was wearing a white housedress that she'd been sleeping in and she was sleepily rubbing her eyes.

Although Parvaneh saw Homa on the stairs, she still wouldn't come in. She just stood in the doorway and talked with Homa.

Within seconds, two men knocked Parvaneh out of the way and

rushed into our home. They ran up the stairs, surrounded my sister and quickly pulled her outside.

Parvaneh cried out, "They arrested Homa!" She left without saying anything. I stood in the doorway, in shock. While standing there, the events of the past few days flashed through my mind. That week, students had set fire to the university president's car. The previous week, the government had given the National Front party permission to hold a peaceful demonstration in a sports arena far from the center of Tehran.

Homa and I went to that gathering with our father. It was the first permitted public demonstration in nine years and I guess we should have been more suspicious for that reason.

Thousands of people came from all over the city to listen while speakers praised the leadership of Dr. Mossadegh. At each mention of his name, the crowd cheered. By the time the third speaker had the floor, the police intervened. They started spraying tear gas into the audience and chasing the crowd in different directions. They were successful in ending what had been a peaceful assembly.

In the confusion, the three of us were separated and I was clubbed with a police stick. The pain was immense. We each ended up scrambling through the streets until we could make it home on our own.

Later that week, students rallied again at the university. The police again responded with force. This time they killed one person and injured four hundred.

It was after this that the president's car was burned. I saw it on my way home as I passed the university. It was awful. The students had taken the car's hubcaps and placed them on top of the pillars of the university gate. As a way of quelling the violence, the government closed the university. It remained shut down for seventy-two days.

Homa had nothing to do with the fire, but she was speaking to a group of demonstrators in front of the medical school that same day. The Savak was after her because of her reputation at the university. Her leadership skills and energy had allowed her to acquire a certain popularity.

In the days following Homa's arrest, our family was frustrated and scared. We were frustrated because we were helpless. We couldn't hire an attorney since no one would take the case. And we couldn't communicate with her at all.

We were scared because we'd heard of the elaborate measures of torture employed by the Savak. During the first few days of her disappearance, our mother could not stop herself from crying. She kept talking about the things they could be doing to her daughter. We were afraid she would be beaten or raped or tortured in some awful way. The thought of my beautiful sister at the mercy of these sick men prevented me from sleeping in those first days.

Our Uncle Hossain tried to use some of his contacts to get information, but he was unsuccessful. We found no trace of Homa. Our father came home from work every night and sat in our living room grinding his teeth. His head would jerk every time he heard the front door open. It was obvious how he waited for her to come home, staring and grinding his teeth. He wouldn't talk much and he didn't listen to his radio. He only sat and waited.

I watched him sometimes, with his grim expression. It looked as though he aged a year every day Homa was gone. It tore me apart to see him that way. I never knew what it meant to have absolutely no control over a situation.

On the fourth day following her capture, one of her classmates came over to tell us what he knew. He said Homa was being held at the Ghasr Prison. He found out that morning from a colleague who was a couple years ahead of him at the medical school. The colleague was also a prison doctor.

Actually, he was a somewhat famous person in Tehran. He'd been a street guard, for most of his youth, and at age thirty he was illiterate. At that point, he decided to become a doctor. After five years he'd educated himself enough to take the entrance exam to the medical school and he passed. He needed to continue working while attending the university and the government assigned him to the prisons. He found Homa on one of his rounds at the Ghasr Prison.

Homa recognized him immediately and asked him to pass a message to us. The message was simple: "Tell my family that I am fine and tell them where I am."

The news came as a giant relief, but we couldn't rejoice too much until we investigated its validity.

The next morning, our mother rushed to the prison to find Homa and to bring her some food and clean clothing. She made this her routine at the start of each day. However, it never provided the relief our family was looking for.

She was never permitted to see her daughter. She would get to the prison and hand over the food and clothing to guards at a gate on the exterior of the holding cells. These guards would feel through the clothing for any foreign material that our mother might have tried to smuggle in. They would also examine the food by sifting through it with metal rods they picked up off the prison floor. It was an awful experience for our mother to have to watch these men work with Homa's belongings in such an aggressive manner. Each time she came back from the prison, she was distraught and angry.

Not being able to see Homa magnified the humility of the ordeal. The tension in our family lessened, but it did not cease. We did not know if Homa was there or if she was safe. We only hoped it was so.

After about two weeks our mother returned from the prison at the usual time, about noon. This time, she was not alone. After two weeks, they allowed her to bring her daughter out of the prison.

Homa's arrival made us all ecstatic. Our father stayed home for the rest of the day and the four of us sat around our living room for lunch and tea. We asked Homa to tell us about her time away. As she did, she was interrupted constantly as friends and relatives who had heard of her release came over to greet her.

She explained that she'd been placed in solitary confinement. They gave her two filthy blankets to keep with her as she slept on the floor of her cell. Over her stay, she was permitted to take two short showers to clean up, and she was given the clean clothing provided by our mother.

Her only friend was the prison doctor, she explained. He smuggled books to her at night. She was grateful for the food our mother had taken her, because the prison meals she had been getting were awful.

Eventually, they questioned her. She described this as the highlight of her captivity.

"I was interviewed by the head of the Savak," she said.

"Really?" I asked excitedly.

"He said, 'Are you Homa Darabi?' and I said 'Yes' but he asked his question as if he was surprised."

"Then what?" our mother asked. We were asking all the questions. Our father barely said a word. He just leaned back and drank the tea. I'm not even sure he was listening. He just stared at Homa and in his eyes was an overwhelming expression of joy.

Homa continued. " 'My goodness!' the man says. 'You're so little! I thought I was meeting Homa Darabi, the powerful woman who makes so much noise at the university.' He says all that, and then I look at him and say, 'Well, now you have!'"

We all laughed.

" 'I see.' he says, and then he starts to ask the tough questions. He wanted to know about the car burning. They asked me if I did it, if I knew who did do it, why it was done? He fired question after question at me, but I refused to answer them all. I just stared across the room at a picture on the wall. It was of the shah."

"You didn't tell them anything?" I asked.

"I only told him that I was free, at the very least, to think what I wanted. My mind is my own and I have the right to promote my thoughts in the absence of violence," she explained.

"What did he say?" I asked.

"He kept asking me questions and I kept telling him that I had a right to speak in public and to voice my own opinions. This went on for another hour, or maybe two. He was so frustrated at the end, he turned to me and said: 'How can such a small girl make such big demands?' I replied, 'Napoleon was also small, and he almost captured the world.' "

We laughed. On the face of it, we couldn't believe her audacity. But none of it truly surprised us. We were just glad to have her back and to hear her speaking to us and to see that she was not harmed.

I always felt that this arrest marked an important time in my own relationship with Homa. When she returned from the prison and told us about the ordeal, I almost felt like I didn't know her. She had become so involved in school. Any free time she had was devoted to her political work. With that, there wasn't much time left for her to spend with me or the family. In fact, her study partner, Mohsen, saw her more than anyone. Her priorities were changing.

Chapter 11

An Enigmatic Decision

Being arrested never stopped Homa from speaking out for what she believed in. As she went through school, she continued to speak at protests on campus and to voice her opinions of current events in Iran.

Still, her life became more secluded than it had been before. Because of the pressures at school, she ended up spending most of her time studying with Mohsen. He had remained a fixture in our household since they helped each other prepare for entrance examinations to the medical school.

I'm not sure when they decided to get married. I don't know why they did, either. To me, Mohsen's presence in our house was a nuisance. Finding time to be alone with my sister was nearly impossible. When they announced their engagement, I didn't know what to say. No one was really surprised, though. They'd been together so often, people were beginning to wonder when it would happen.

But I questioned the decision. They just seemed too different. I thought that Mohsen had little in common with my sister, but I wasn't sure how much of an impact he'd made on her after spending so much time with her for four years. Maybe she wanted to change.

Still, there were obvious clashes in their personalities. Some of these arose when they planned their wedding. Homa wanted a big wedding to be held in the presence of all her friends and family. She wanted to be dressed in a gorgeous white gown and to be the most beautiful woman in the crowd. But Mohsen preferred an intimate wedding that could take place in someone's home and in the presence of only the immediate family.

Our mother noticed these conflicts. She sometimes confronted Homa about them. "How in the world are you going to live a life with this man if the two of you can't even agree on simple wedding arrangements?!"

"If there's a problem, I'll ask for a divorce," Homa would reply.

"Sweetheart, things are not as easy as you think. Marriage is a life-time commitment. Once you enter it, you don't have the freedom to walk out on it."

"I will! Once I get the right to divorce, I can leave him if I have to."

Conversations like this happened frequently during the engage-ment. Their arguments used to get quite heated.

The first time I really feared for my sister's happiness, though, occurred when I bought tickets to a concert for Homa, our mother, and Mohsen. My sister decided to dress up that night. She wore a red dress that was open around the neck and had thin straps that wrapped around her shoulders. That night I remember how exquisite her soft olive skin looked against the red satin fabric of the gown. She styled her black hair in a way so that her high cheekbones would be accented. She even used a bit more makeup than usual. I thought she looked stunning.

However, when Mohsen came to our house that night, he was dis-pleased with the sight of his fiancée. He became distraught and demanded that she wash her face and change her outfit.

My sister refused, and an argument broke out. I saw Mohsen slap Homa with an open hand and grab her to make her obey him.

Our mother did not like seeing her daughter beaten by her fiancé and so she intervened and ordered Mohsen to leave.

Appalled by her action, he screamed at his future mother-in-law. "Your daughter is my responsibility now and you should stay out of our affairs!" He left the house, slamming the door behind him.

After he left, I looked at Homa. She was crying, and I was frightened for her. Mohsen rarely spoke to me when he came to our house and I didn't especially like him, but I never knew he could be violent.

A few minutes passed and then our mother turned to Homa and began attacking her verbally. "Didn't you know that this would be his reaction?! Why would you want to start such an argument?! You could have just worn your normal clothes! Look at your sister and me, we haven't dressed up at all! Why would you want to cause so much trouble?! You should know better!"

Homa took her anger toward Mohsen and directed it at our mother. "What the hell is wrong with you people?! All I did was dress nice! So what, I looked good, nobody gives a damn. Why should you?!"

The argument went in circles, and eventually our mother was pleading with her daughter to think twice about the idea of marrying her fiancé.

"Homa, sweetheart, please. Think about this. Break this engagement! This man is not going to treat you right. He's just like your father."

"But mother, who does?! What man in this country can treat a woman right?! Show me one!"

"Homa, you are earning a degree and you will be a doctor soon. You can find a better husband. You can find one to appreciate you! Times are changing and not all men abuse their wives. It isn't expected of them anymore."

But my sister's answer was always the same. "If something happens and things go bad I will divorce him. I'll ask for the right to divorce as a condition of our marriage. Things will change after we get married and finish our education. Mohsen is different now. He's under too much pressure at school. Things will change. He will change. I will change him and make him accept my standards."

Our mother, of course, was afraid the man would never change.

Homa invested a lot of her future in the idea that she would one day have the right to divorce anyone she married. She thought she could use such a right as protection in case anything went wrong with her marriage. It was a kind of safety net for her.

But in Iran and other Islamic countries, women are not given such a right automatically. They must ask for it at the time of marriage. But even when such power is granted, it is not easy for women to petition for divorce. The right, in fact, is almost entirely reserved for men.

Under Islam, a man can divorce his wife without ever explaining anything to her. He decides on his own. On the other hand, a woman who has secured the right to divorce as part of her marriage contract must work with the courts. This makes the process a long and time-consuming one.

Homa did not recognize the diluted meaning of the right to divorce. She placed a blind faith in it and this is what caused the principle dispute between her and our mother. Our mother knew how one-sided the country's divorce laws were. She thought they were unjust. She placed little faith in a woman's right to divorce. In her mind it didn't make sense to marry a man if you already thought about the possibility of having to divorce one day. She eventually had to give in to the wishes of her daughter, however. She knew that Homa had a mind of her own.

Why Homa decided to marry this man is its own mystery. When she was young, she never liked to talk about her personal life. We didn't know what she thought of men. There was a time, however, when she had fallen in love with someone. And in those months, she couldn't hide her feelings from anyone.

When my sister was seventeen, we spent the summer with our Uncle Hossain in the northern part of Iran, along the Caspian Sea. While there, Homa met a young man named Keyvan. He was tall and had dark skin and dark eyes. He was a friend of our uncle's.

As soon as Keyvan saw Homa, he began to pursue her. He tried his best to get her attention. Within a few days Homa responded and the two started spending most of their time together.

In those times, young people were allowed to be with each other only if they were chaperoned. Our uncle did not mind the idea of his niece getting together with his friend and so Homa was free to fall in love with this young man.

During the day, they spent time at the beach, near the sea with the rest of us. At night we used to gather in our uncle's home. Friends and family would come from around the area. But the one constant at all of these parties was that Homa and Keyvan would be together. They were almost inseparable and everyone knew it.

If there were moments when Homa was alone that summer, we would all tease her by asking where Keyvan was. Why wasn't he with her? She hated the teasing but there was nothing she could do. She was falling in love with him.

Uncle Hossain's wife said it best once when preparing dinner in the kitchen while Homa was in the other room with her new friend. "They're in love," she said.

"Oh, now, come on!" Hossain scoffed. "What are you talking about? They are children having fun. No one speaks of love."

"But Hossain, dear, I can see it."

"What do you see, Giti? Do you see hearts where their eyes should be?! Do you see their names written on the moon, or in tea leaves? What do you see?" He was emphatic. I was laughing at the sight of our uncle having fun with his wife.

But Giti did not give in. Her husband's antics made her smirk, but she said it again. "They're in love, and I can see it in their eyes when they dance."

Her statement subdued everyone. We were all serious again and Uncle Hossain said nothing. We stood quietly until someone changed the subject.

Throughout the summer, Homa and Keyvan spent time together and became close. They used to wake up early in order to watch the sun rise and then they would stay out until they could watch it set.

One morning, when we were alone, I asked Homa about him.

"How's Keyvan?"

"He's fine."

"How are you?"

"I'm fine."

"How are you and Keyvan?" I was trying not to laugh.

"Stop it!"

"Stop what?"

She didn't want to respond anymore. She tried to ignore me.

"What do the two of you do all day?" She still wasn't responding. "I saw you both on the beach with books. Why did you have books?"

"We were reading." She said it in a sour tone, but she was beginning to smile.

"Reading? What do you read?"

"Poetry."

"Poetry?"

"And stories, short stories. You know, like Poe and Chekhov."

"Oh, right." My smile grew as I paused. "So does he read them to you, or do you both read silently and then talk about them?"

"Shut up!"

"No, I'm serious. Who reads?"

She was reluctant to answer but when I asked again she told me. "We both read. Sometime he does, and sometimes I do. It depends on who finds the story. It's no big deal."

"Sounds romantic. You think some day I might find someone to read with?" Oh, that made her mad. I don't think we ever teased Homa as much as we did that summer. It was easy though, because she was so happy in those days. I mean, she was glowing. You never saw her without a smile.

The rest of the family was almost as happy as she was. They knew that Homa's friend was from a well-to-do family. Our family always looked to Homa for that. They knew that Homa was beautiful enough to attract the kind of man who could have everything. As she grew older, in fact, they began to rely on her for some kind of upward mobility.

She was a kind of investment in that respect. But I never thought of it as unfair or improper. Homa was just that kind of girl. She was so beautiful that if she hadn't been taken care of, it would have been a crime. It made sense to them that Keyvan would fall in love with Homa because of her beauty and then ignore the fact that her family was from a financially lower class.

Once the summer ended, the romance continued when Keyvan was invited to every family gathering we had. Their relationship stayed strong and they continued to grow closer.

Sometime after that, he called on Homa and asked her to walk with him on Pahlavi Avenue. In those days Pahlavi Avenue was the most romantic place in Tehran. It was a wide strip with walkways on either side and small canals that lined the paths. There were Asian oak trees which kept the street shady. It was, and still is, one of the main thoroughfares in Tehran. In the northern suburb of Shemiran, beneath the Alborz Mountains, the street begins and it slopes downward throughout the city. Water from the snow-covered peaks constantly flows in the canals along the street. The sound of the rushing waters adds to the romance.

During the day, we were all very nervous for Homa because we expected Keyvan to propose. But she wasn't gone long and when she came back, she ran straight to her room and closed the door behind her. From the kitchen, we could hear her crying.

Mother and I rushed after her to find out what went wrong. With her head burrowed into her pillow, she tried to stop crying long enough to explain what had happened.

"What happened, sweetheart, didn't he propose?" My mother asked, even though she already knew that the proposal hadn't come. She didn't know what else to say.

"No! he didn't. He didn't want me." She spoke in short sentences that were interrupted by tears. "He said it was Daddy. Daddy wasn't rich. He wanted a girl with a father in high places. Our father is nothing. He's a homebuilder. But he said he loved me!"

She continued to cry and her screams only got louder. We just stayed next to her. It was shocking. We were all humiliated.

Plenty of young men would have given everything they had for just a smile from my sister. But once her heart was broken, she might have been too scared to let go of her emotions with someone new. Mohsen was safe to her. He didn't play games and she knew he'd never run away. He didn't mind the financial status of our family either. Maybe when he came around, she saw life with him as a logical, safe choice.

Still, I'm not sure I can rationalize Homa's decision to marry in that way. There must have been more to it. I know, because my sister never made decisions without tremendous forethought. She was a meticulous decision maker. It was something that placed Homa in a category with our mother. They were methodical people who never liked to make quick choices and felt uncomfortable taking risks.

Homa had a difficult time choosing things when she was faced with variety. She believed that the only way to make an appropriate decision was to evaluate each option one by one. If she went shopping with Mother, it would take them days to find the right fabric. It wasn't because she was searching for the perfect combination of color and material. It was because she felt as though she should make sure she knew of all the available fabrics in the bazaar.

Once she found the right fabric, she would then end up spending hours with her tailor. She had to search through every journal the tailor had before she could decide on the design she wanted.

When people gave her things, she had a much easier time. Any time she could avoid having to make decisions, she was happier. When it was time for her to marry, it was easy because Mohsen chose her.

One thing about her decisions, though, she stuck with them. She was stubborn in that way. Once she made up her mind, she never wavered.

Chapter 12

A Wedding with Obstacles

Homa and Mohsen were engaged for almost three years. Their first wedding date was set for the summer of 1962. But a few weeks before the event, an aunt of ours started having problems with her gallbladder.

For help, she came to Homa, and Homa took her to the hospital where she was in training. They operated on our aunt's gallbladder there, but the surgery was botched when the surgeon sliced through one of her veins. Apparently, he could not find the vein to sew it up and our aunt bled to death.

Homa stayed with her during the operation, but she left once our aunt had been taken from the recovery room and placed in the ward. I remember when Homa came home that evening. She was very nervous. She helped our mother with dinner, but she wouldn't eat.

In the evening, a messenger came from the hospital with the bad news. He told us that our aunt was bleeding internally and that she had gone into a coma.

Homa and I rushed with our mother to the hospital and when we got there our aunt was being operated on a second time. Homa was allowed in the operating room.

By 2:30 A.M., Homa came out to the waiting room. She had a sick look on her face and dried tears around her eyes. She said the doctors had tried their best to find the broken vein, but the artery was lost within the fat tissues. As soon as we saw Homa's face, we knew our aunt was gone and that Homa had lost her first patient.

The next day we had to inform her children of her death. An Islamic mourning process began, and Homa's wedding was to be postponed for an entire year. By religious standards, celebrating joyful events during the year after a close relative dies is considered a sign of disrespect.

After the anniversary of our aunt's death, Homa and Mohsen set a new date for their wedding on one of the Moslem holy days. After much anxiety and several fights Homa was able to plan the wedding her way. She made arrangements to rent a large hall so that she could invite everyone she wanted. She also purchased fabric for a beautiful white gown that was then tailored perfectly to the contours of her body.

In Iran, the groom's family is expected to bear the costs of the wedding and the bride must bring a decent dowry for the newlyweds to live on. But because Homa and Mohsen were both students and could not afford to support themselves, they made plans to stay with our family until they finished their education.

Planning a successful wedding and having a successful wedding are two different things, however. Sure enough, about a month prior to their wedding, problems arose again. This time the problem originated in the groom's family.

Mohsen had a grandfather who was very old. He became sick and was forced to stay in a hospital in the days preceding the scheduled wedding of his grandson. With two weeks left until the wedding day, the grandfather announced to his family that he could predict his death. He said he was going to die on the upcoming Moslem holy day—the day of his grandson's wedding ceremony.

After this announcement, Homa and Mohsen panicked. They did not want to see this man die on the day of their wedding, because it would have been an awful combination of events. They also feared the possibility of his dying before the marriage because that would postpone their wedding for another year.

The solution to them was simple. They canceled all their previous plans and decided to get married as soon as possible. However, it wasn't the only solution suggested. Most everyone saw the first delay of their wedding as a tragic coincidence. Now, though, people were beginning to question the role fate might play in the delays.

Our grandmother has a niece named Parisa. She is the most religious woman in our family. She has a great faith in God and is also a superstitious person.

When she heard of the groom's grandfather's illness and of his prediction, she consulted my sister and tried to make her see things in a different light. "Homa, pay attention to what is happening around you. Do you see the meaning behind it?"

"What are you talking about, Parisa? I'm getting married soon. Why do you want to bring up subjects like this? You know I don't see things as you do. I never have. Why would I now?"

"But Homa, you are my cousin and my friend, and I want you to make the right choices in your life. I only worry for you because you only see things as they are. You do not look beneath the surface to what they could be."

"There is no sense in seeing things as they could be, it is too much trouble and it means nothing. I have seen people waste their thoughts on such matters and I can only tell you that I have no thoughts to spare. My mind is too busy just worrying about things the way they are."

"Homa, I know this about you. Your mind works fast and you have a lot to think about. Clearly, you do not have the time to waste your thoughts, but I believe that your thoughts on this particular matter would not be wasted. I believe that God is talking to you."

Homa rolled her eyes. "Why would God want to talk to me? Look around at the world. Have you been to the hospital lately? Look at all the people God has to talk to in there. He has no time for me."

"God *has* time for you."

"Okay, then, fine. What does God say to me? What does he want to tell me? What have I done wrong?"

"I do not believe that you have done anything wrong. But I think that you are ignoring him."

"I have heard no words from God lately."

"He doesn't speak with words, he uses actions. His actions are more subtle than words. They leave you the freedom of interpretation. He knows that you must think for yourself."

"So what is it then? What's he trying to say to me. What am I doing wrong?" She was growing impatient.

"The death of your aunt and the sickness of your fiancé's grandfather are his messages. God must have told the old man that he would die on that date, the day of your wedding. These things can mean only one thing. You're not supposed to marry this man. You should call the wedding off, completely."

"Thank you, Parisa, are you done? May I go on with my life now? The wedding will be soon. Please come, but I don't want to see you before then, okay?"

Homa was never very close with her spiritual side. She didn't believe in any of it. She probably thought Parisa was too religious. Actually most of us felt that way about Parisa. She used to speak of God as if he were a friend living down the street.

Homa laughed at those who claimed a higher power was trying to prevent her marriage. She saw everything as coincidence and she saw no more than bad luck involved in the delays.

I have always felt the same way about these kinds of superstitions. As time went on, though, Parisa continued to restate her belief that God disapproved of my sister's bond to her husband. I never took her seriously until the last time I heard her say it, over the phone, on the day of Homa's funeral.

It brought a chill to me.

Homa decided to move her wedding date one week forward. In order to inform the guests of the changed date, we had to make calls to our friends and family. We also spent time making personal visits to many of the guests because they did not own phones.

The guest list was divided between our mother, Aunt Maryam, Uncle Hossain, Aunt Pari, and myself. Our Aunt Masoumeh had a phone and I learned about a further change after talking with her.

"Good morning, Aunt Masoumeh. This is Parvin. How are you?"

"Oh, Parvin, I'm just fine. How are things with you?"

"Well, I'm real busy because we moved Homa's wedding day up to Friday and I have to call the guests to let them know.

"Friday? Are you sure? You know your mother called me a few hours ago and she said the wedding was planned for Wednesday."

"Really?" I asked, not believing what I heard.

"She said you were having it at your house."

"That's strange because I thought it was Friday. I better find out."

"Well, your mother said it was being brought forward because the groom's grandfather's condition was getting worse."

"Yeah, that's why we wanted to have the wedding on Friday."

"Right, well, I guess he's gotten worse."

"Really?" Now I was starting to understand the confusion.

"Your mother said the doctors are worried because they think the gentleman could die any minute. She wanted to move the date forward again. I think she wanted me to tell you when you called."

It made sense. I had been at work all day and there was no way for Mother to communicate with me. She called Aunt Masoumeh, knowing that I would call her, and left the message for me.

A wedding on Wednesday, however, meant a wedding in three days. I ended up taking the next two days off from work to help with the arrangements. For the rest of the evening I chartered a taxi to take me around the city so that I could inform the guests of the second change.

That was a tough job. At each home, I had to come in, drink a cup of tea, and eat something. Not only did everyone want to know the new date, but they also had to hear the story behind the changes. I don't even know what time I got home that night.

When I did arrive, I was tired. Sleep was out of the question, though. We had too much to do. We had to prepare the house to host a wedding of glamorous proportions in less than three days.

By the time we were through, we had created a gorgeous environment despite the constraints. The house was wired up with colorful lights that lit up the bushes and marked the frame of the house. We placed a record player outside in the yard and spread Persian rugs over the tile. We needed chairs for people to sit on and we borrowed those from our neighbors.

For food, the three sisters—Maryam, Mother, and Pari—worked in the kitchen for the entire time. Several friends also came to help them. Mother also worked on what would be the ceremonial room, where they arranged Homa's *sofreh aghd.*

This was the most memorable part of the preparations. Homa and I listened to Mother become sentimental. She spent hours with us telling stories from her own wedding and explaining how much things had changed since then.

"I was so young. You know, I was only thirteen when they married me to your father. And I didn't know him. Marriage was just different back then. And now, two decades later so much has changed.

"Homa, you're twenty-three. When I was young, people would have said you were too old to marry. Isn't that something? You've had the chance to meet your husband and you even picked him. The engagement went on for years so you had time to think about it."

She laughed a little. "I never had time to think. I wasn't expected to think. My mother had done the thinking for me. She figured a girl at thirteen couldn't possibly understand what was best for herself and so she made those decisions for me."

Mother took her attention away from the *sofreh* and looked directly at her daughter. "You, sweetheart, are so different. You're grown and educated and you are old enough to accept responsibility for your own life." She worked for a while before she started to speak again.

"There used to be musicians. If you wanted to have a wedding, you had to hire people to play the music. The musicians were glorious showmen. They would wear colorful outfits and entertain the crowd with a stage show."

"Now they've all been replaced by our record player. Can you imagine what went into that little box? How many musicians have been taken from their trade? Now they don't need to entertain crowds—they just make records."

What mother did not talk about, were the things that hadn't changed. Tradition dictated the ceremony. Divorced or widowed women were not allowed as guests in the bride's room. Men, of course, were not permitted either. The groom and the other men were to stay out in the yard while the ceremony proceeded.

At the completion of the wedding ceremony, Homa would become the property of her husband. For the rest of their lives together, she would have to obey him. Anything she wanted to do or any decisions she wanted to make about her career or her future would require his endorsement. Technology had changed and the role of women in society had developed, but tradition was stubborn.

On the day of the wedding, the guests were the first people to arrive. When they came, the women gathered upstairs in the bride's room and the men outside in the front yard. Then Mohsen and his family arrived and they brought the *mullah* with them to perform the ceremony.

Homa spent the afternoon at a beauty parlor. She was the last to arrive. I remember how beautiful she looked that evening. Her floor-length white wedding gown was actually out of place in the small room we had. It had a long cape that fell from her back and it had to be pulled forward and held on the sides by safety pins. The dress was more suited for a formal wedding. I wore a green satin dress that had been made for me a year earlier, prior to the original wedding date.

There was something about this event that didn't feel right. The sight of Homa with her glorious dress stuffed into a tiny room seemed to set an eerie mood.

I'm not sure if anyone there felt good about the marriage. Even Homa acted a little apprehensive. To me, it seemed as though she was performing a duty rather than starting a new life.

Marriage in Iran was and still is an expectation. Girls simply had to be married before they turned twenty-five, or they would be ostracized by society. If they hadn't married by then, something must be wrong with them. They would be considered old maids and be pitied by other women.

There is a custom in a Persian wedding very similar to the Western tradition of throwing the bouquet. At the end of the wedding ceremony, all of the items that are laid on the *sofreh aghd* are removed from the cloth, which is then shaken over the heads of girls who are single but are old enough to be married. When the time comes to perform this ritual, the older ladies always end up searching out each of the so-called old maids in the room so they can participate. After all, they need it the most, right?

The experience can be quite humiliating for these older women who have supposedly grown too old to be married. Our Aunt Maryam was frequently a victim of this humiliation. We watched it happen to her at every wedding for years. She would be the only woman over thirty sitting under the shaking of the *sofreh aghd* with teenagers. But Homa's wedding was memorable because it didn't happen to Maryam there. Maryam had finally been married.

A year after her father died, Maryam was working at Bimarestan-e-Sina, one of the university hospitals. There, she met a medical student, an intern, and fell in love with him. But, she was not confident about their future together because they came from dissimilar backgrounds.

The man was poor and from one of the villages in Iran. He expected to use his medical education as a passport to instant upward mobility. He wanted to find a wealthy wife from a well-known family.

Maryam knew that she could not fulfill this role and when the family made arrangements for her to marry another gentleman, she agreed. He was a young man with a decent future as a pharmacist. He ran his own business, as our father did. He seemed to really be in love with Maryam, even though it was an arranged marriage.

Everything was settled between the two families and all that was left to be done was to plan the wedding. But before they could make these plans, the man Maryam loved, the intern, came to her and begged her to call off her engagement to the pharmacist.

I don't know the details of what happened next but they never got married. Maryam has never been willing to talk about it, but I believe the intern lied to her and left her standing at the altar.

He begged her not to go through with her marriage to the pharmacist and promised to marry her immediately. In fact, he told Maryam that he would marry her within ten days of their talk.

She came home, that day, and stayed in her room for most of the evening. When she finally came out, she called off her engagement to the pharmacist.

We all felt very badly for the pharmacist. Homa and I were young and we had never seen a man cry before. The pharmacist came to Maryam's and begged her to change her mind and marry him, and he wept pitifully. She refused to do so.

When it was time for the pharmacist to leave, he turned to Maryam and asked God to make her as miserable in her love life as she had made him on that evening.

Maryam was a beautiful woman with blonde hair and green eyes. These are very uncommon colors in Iran. She was also taller than most women in Iran. Her legs were long and her skin soft and smooth when she was young. But it wasn't enough. She needed more to get the man she loved to marry her.

The intern wanted to use his degree as a stepping stone to money and fame. Aunt Maryam's family could not provide either. The men in our family were only average businessmen with no money and fame. Such professions carried little weight with the more prominent circles in Iran.

Words are strong tools and faith is something people are suckers for, but, eventually, the curse came true. Ten days turned into a month and the month into a year. Five years later, the intern married a woman from a family that could give him social prominence and fortune. He had told Maryam there was no instant fame and fortune in love and there was no reason for both of them to live in poverty. How wrong he was.

Maryam was to be the oldest woman under the *sofreh aghd* at every wedding our family attended. She finally married a man, out of desperation, while she was in her mid-thirties. That wedding preceded Homa's by a few months. But she was alone again, months later, after a bitter divorce.

Life was not so easy for the medical student either. Over time, he stayed in touch with our family. He ended up with two sons of his own, but his heart never let go of our aunt.

Homa used to say society did it to them. She said society condemned the two of them. She was angry at something but I didn't understand what. Anyway, she talked about our aunt. "It's just awful for both of them. Neither one of them has had a happy life. You can tell because neither one of them has forgotten the other. They had love—real love. But they put it aside because the rest of the world doesn't put much stock in the idea of love. Marriage isn't about love around here. When you see them today, they both look like they realize their mistakes.

"They might have been happier if they'd just ignored the whole world and stuck together. But they couldn't. Here, they couldn't."

I cut her off. "But, Homa, they should have. The doctor should have had more confidence in his abilities as a surgeon. He should have realized that he didn't need to look for a wealthy father-in-law to find success in his own life."

"But Parvin, you just don't understand these things because you are young, and you aren't knowledgeable about people. It is society that makes the rules. Society forces a young man to sell his soul for upward mobility. The two of them were left with no alternative but to follow the rules. There was no other option for either of them."

"God! What kind of a place have we built for ourselves?"

I often wonder if Homa ever worried that she might end up being the woman over whom the *sofreh aghd* is shaken at weddings. Regardless, by 7 P.M. of the day of her wedding, Homa had said yes and she was Mohsen's wife from that day forward.

As it turned out, Mohsen's grandfather died on the day he predicted. Our father paid for the entire wedding and the newlyweds moved into our house the next day.

I hated the way Mohsen acted while he lived in our home. He had to be taken care of by our mother and father. They cooked for Mohsen and Homa and cleaned up after them while they continued going to school.

The air inside our house in those days seemed thick and tense. I fought with my sister a lot in those days. In fact, I fought with almost everyone back then. It was hard for me. I used to be able to go home to rest after a day of work, but now I had no place to use for any kind of escape. There was just too much tension at home. I hated seeing our parents reduced to servants for this individual my sister had given her freedom to.

To get away from this situation, I spent most of my time at work preparing to leave for America. I was trying to fulfill my dream to leave Iran by saving enough money to take care of myself.

Chapter 13

A Long-Awaited Departure

In 1963, the government of Iran ratified the Family Protection Act which banned polygamy and the unilateral right of men to divorce. Additionally, laws which hindered women's rights were, in practice, ignored. This was a significant step forward for the women of Iran. Yet, equality was still a long way away.

Around the same time, I came home on a Thursday afternoon after spending the morning at work and found Mother waiting for me.

"I've arranged your appointments at the public bath and the beauty shop. So eat something quickly and go there."

I had a routine of my own in those days and it involved bathing on Thursdays. Usually, though, I went to the public bath and waited in line for a few hours. My mother had never made any kind of reservation for me before. Naturally, I was suspicious. "That's nice of you, but why?"

She didn't answer me and so I went to get cleaned up. When I came back in the evening, I found Homa with our Aunt Maryam preparing hors d'oeuvres.

"What's going on?" I asked.

"Nothing," Homa said. "We're just having some guests."

"Who?"

"We don't know them. Some friends of Maryam introduced them."

"It's a *khastegar*, isn't it—a matchmaker?!" I was very angry.

In Iran, the process of courting is called *khastegary*. It is a system of pairing couples through arranged engagements put together by the families.

The process usually begins when a young man advertises his availability. Then, the rest of the community begins searching for an appropriate match. Passive, quiet young ladies are preferred, and relative youth is a must.

Once found, the bachelor's female relatives visit the family of the prospective bride. Here, the young woman is expected to serve tea while she is under the strict scrutiny of her guests. This was the objective of tonight's gathering. I was to be scrutinized by people I didn't even know.

It can be a humiliating experience. When Homa and I were a few years younger, we sat with our mother and her sisters after they'd returned from a *khastegary* for our uncle. It was appalling, the way they spoke about the young woman they'd just been with.

"I think her nose was too big," our mother said.

"It's true," our aunt agreed. "And did you notice her eyebrows? They were so thick."

Homa found the discussion particularly disturbing and she had to interrupt. "Enough! The girl is human! You can't expect her to be perfect. She is not a fabric or a piece of furniture. Don't treat her like one!"

After the females of the family meet with the young woman, and approve her, the rest of the groom's family must also meet with her family. If they also approve, all that remains is to discuss the *mehryeh* —a symbol of the girl's monetary value.

The negotiation can go on for days and it often ends in disagreement. Homa once came home from the university with an article she found in the paper. A man was offering his daughter to her prospective suitor, if he could simply provide him with her weight in gold.

"Can you imagine how humiliating this is?!" Homa once told me. "It's as if he is asking for a ransom. A young girl should not be for sale. She is a person. She should be able to marry whoever she wants."

Indeed, our family was a fairly liberal one. Therefore, I was shocked to learn that my own loved ones had compromised their own values for my sake.

I refused to serve the tea.

Shortly after that, I left Iran for the United States, on February 7, 1964, with a one-way plane ticket and five hundred U.S. dollars.

Homa and Mohsen spent their time keeping up with school and working a few hours each week trying to sell medical products to doctors. They made enough money to pay their day-to-day expenses, but they still had to live with our parents.

In 1965, they graduated. Homa gave birth to a baby girl. She named her Azita. After graduation, Iranian law dictated that new doctors spend two years practicing medicine outside of Tehran. Mohsen had to spend the time as a military doctor and Homa moved to northern Iran to open a small private practice. This was the first time they were able to live alone.

By February 1968 they had passed the United States Foreign Medical Graduates Educational Council's exam in Tehran and were qualified to continue their education in the United States. Shortly after, they moved to America.

By 1968, I had been married for almost a year, to an American named Robert Thomson. I was in engineering school at California State University Northridge, and I worked to pay my expenses. My schedule left little time for rest. Coming home in the evening after work was always a gratifying feeling. But I remember it as a slow walk.

On an August evening, in Conoga Park, California, I was walking up the front steps to the home my husband and I were renting when I heard the phone ringing.

I hurried inside and grabbed the receiver that hung on our wall in the kitchen. "Hello?"

"Parvin! How are you?!"

"Oh my God, I don't believe it. Homa! What are you doing, where are you?" I knew she couldn't have been calling from Iran because the reception was too clear.

"We're in Bethesda, Maryland. We just got here from Iran and I wanted to call and see how you were doing."

"I'm so glad you called. It is so wonderful to hear your voice. God, how long has it been?"

"Really, too long."

"Well, wait a minute, what are you doing in Bethesda? You could have come to California."

"We want to get residency here, because it takes less time. Maryland makes life easier on its doctors."

"Wow, I can't believe you guys are out here. Isn't it amazing? We're so far from home right now."

"I know, but we passed our test and the government let us in. Now we just have to figure out what we want to do from here."

"Where's Mohsen, is he with you? How is he?"

"He's fine, and he's here with me. We're renting an apartment here in Bethesda."

"What about your daughter? How is she?"

"She's great."

"And what about Mom and Dad?"

"They're fine, too. They're both back home, but Mother is going to come out here to see us."

"Oh wow! It's amazing. I can't believe we're both here. You know, it's a long way from home. I have so many things to ask you about. I don't know where to begin. What are our grandmothers doing?"

"Oh . . . well, Parvin, Aziz is fine, but, don't you know? Madar died almost two years ago."

Madar was our father's mother.

"What? How?!" I loved Madar. We always got on well together.

"She caught a bad cold and Dad brought her home to live with us. One morning she didn't wake up. But she died in her sleep without pain. This happened about two years ago. I guess you didn't know?"

"No! No one told me. No one said a thing. Mom wrote me and she always said Madar was fine. I can't believe this." I was confused. The family had hid this from me for two years!

"Oh, Parvin, I'm so sorry. I know how much you loved her."

"But why didn't someone tell me? How could you people keep me in the dark like this? What were you thinking?!"

"I guess Mom and Dad didn't want to upset you. We're all so worried about you in a strange country all by yourself."

"But that's no excuse! It bothers me still, hearing about it now! It bothers me more!" I was furious and I knew I shouldn't keep talking to Homa in this mood.

"I'm sorry, Parvin."

"I have to go. I mean, I want to talk to you, Homa, but I should go. I can't talk like this. I need to think things over for a while. I'll call you in a few days. What's your number?" She gave it to me and I thanked her and hung up.

My family does strange things. They're too protective. I felt betrayed by them. It took me a few days to digest what had happened.

I used to keep the letters my mother sent me in a box in the bedroom closet. I pulled it out after talking with Homa and started reading through the letters. Each one of them included details about the health of my deceased grandmother. She never failed to mention her. They knew what she meant to me and they were afraid to tell me the truth about her. I felt foolish.

There was no reason for them to be that way. You can't protect someone from the sad events of life. Eventually, I would find out she was dead, right? It's better to be up front with someone.

Within a short time, I wanted to talk with my sister again. I calmed down and tried the phone again.

"Hello?"

I could hear static on the line while she spoke. "Homa? It's me, how are you?"

"We're fine! I'm glad you called." She was excited. "You know, we're starting to get things settled around here. We've just arranged to start our internship in a month at the local hospital. We have an apartment now, and it's furnished. The only thing we haven't done is figure out what to do about our daughter. We need someone to take care of her while we work."

"Yeah, you'll both be working long hours. You should hire an au pair."

"Well, I talked to Mom." She was hesitating. "I asked her to come live with us for a while. She could really help us out."

"What, are you nuts?! Mom lives in Iran. What the hell is she going to do with herself in Bethesda? And what about Dad? Did you ask him, too? How's he going to leave his business?"

"We didn't ask him. We can't really afford to take care of both of them and besides, Mom and Dad don't really get along anymore. They barely communicate when they are home together. Their relationship was awful when you were around, but since you left it's only gotten worse."

What she said made me sad. I imagined what it must have been like back home. My poor father and mother having to look after their daughter, son-in-law, and their grandchild.

If their relationship had really decayed, it's understandable. Our mother and father never really had a good relationship and to burden them with all this work was unfair.

But now my parents were alone.

Homa kept pressing. "You know if Dad stays alone in Iran, it's good for him. He can do his own thing for a while. I mean, in a year the internship will be complete and then Mom can go back to him. It's not a permanent thing."

"But Homa, it's just not right. You can't separate them. You should just let them alone for a while."

"Parvin, you just don't know. They don't communicate. It's not healthy for them to even be together. I think it's a good idea to separate them for a while."

I was trying to tell her that I thought her marriage was killing our parent's relationship. But there didn't seem to be a way to do it tactfully. It was clear, too, that Homa wasn't going to believe such an idea.

"Homa, why don't you just hire an au pair? Bring someone in the house to care for your kid. You know our parents have lived together for over thirty years and if you leave them alone they'll continue to do so. Why would you want to throw their life away? Hire an au pair. It's a far better solution."

"Mom says she doesn't want to live with Dad without us around."

This angered me. I felt it was a lie. I thought Homa was just coming up with an argument to justify what she wanted to do. She didn't care about the truth of her statements.

"What about the au pair?!" I challenged her to come up with an excuse that would make hiring someone impossible.

The blame fell on her husband. "Mohsen doesn't want our daughter to be raised by a stranger."

"An au pair wouldn't raise your children, they just clean up after them—"

"But the time! They spend all that time with the children and make a major impact on their lives. We shouldn't allow a stranger to do that to our own daughter. We should make the time for her. Look at us, the way we were raised. We were surrounded by family. I want to give that environment to my daughter."

"But Homa, this is America. Children are raised differently here. They don't need to be surrounded by family all the time. Besides, it would be impossible to surround her here anyway. We don't have enough family in the United States."

"That's no excuse to allow strangers to raise your children."

"People do it all the time."

"Well, Mohsen wouldn't stand for it. He believes it's wrong and I agree with him. We have to raise our daughter. It's our responsibility."

"Wait a minute! What about him? What about his parents? Why don't they come out to help?"

"It's different."

"Different! How is it different?"

"The child is mine. It's my responsibility. I have to find someone to care for it and it can't be a stranger. Mohsen says it has to be family—either our mother or you. That's the only way—unless I want to give up my career and stay home for a couple of years."

The conversation had just become crazy. I couldn't believe what I was hearing. "What kind of an attitude is that?! You're supposed to be married. Who the hell decided it was your job to raise the kid? You guys are supposed to help each other. And what the hell do you mean our mother or me?! I have a life, too, you know. Did you think about that?"

"Of course I did. That's why I made arrangements with our mother. I knew you wouldn't want to come out here. Mohsen just thought you might. He thought we could pay for your schooling and you could take care of our daughter."

"Forget it! Don't even think about it! I'm married, and I'm

working my way through school. I can't just drop everything and come take care of your little girl. It would be impossible."

"Well, you and Mom are our only two options."

I calmed down a little and thought of an idea. "Homa, why don't you send your daughter to Iran and let her stay there with our parents and then bring her back after you complete your internship program. That way she can be raised by the whole family back home."

But she was resistant. "No, that wouldn't be right. It wouldn't be fair to Azita. Our daughter needs to know who her parents are. She needs to spend time with us."

"I thought you were telling me that you and your husband need to spend thirty-six hours at the hospital for every twelve at home. When are you going to see your child?"

"During those twelve hours."

"Homa, this is selfish. You shouldn't break up Mom and Dad for your own sake. Please don't do it. I beg you."

She finally abandoned her defensive tone and conceded something. "I know. I don't really want to break them up, but I don't know what else to do. If I don't go on with the internship, my career may never take off. I'll never achieve my dream. It just seems like this is only temporary and it will work out okay. I only need her for a couple of years."

"I don't understand that husband of yours. It's like he wants you to fail. If he wanted a homemaker then why did he marry a medical student? He could have learned from his brothers. They are almost all married to homemakers, aren't they?"

We ended our conversation and I felt sorry for Homa. She was trapped. She wanted to practice medicine more than anything else and all of a sudden she found herself compromised because she had a child. I knew how stubborn she was. Our whole family is incredibly stubborn. She'd made her mind up about bringing our mother over before we'd talked. Nothing I could say was going to change that. Arguing anymore would have been futile.

After we hung up, I stayed in the kitchen and started making dinner. It was a tough conversation. I hadn't seen my sister for four years since leaving Iran in 1964. When I left, I was beginning to sense the crumbling of our relationship. Our recent conversations did not help the situation.

We had argued a lot during the last year I was living in Iran. I spent most of my time making plans for what I would do with myself once I escaped to America. The two of us could never see eye-to-eye on most subjects and that was driving us apart.

Now, our differences were as clear as ever. Our sisterhood was in jeopardy. The conversation about my mother was just the beginning. I felt strongly that our parents should not have their life together, even if they were unhappy, destroyed because Mohsen didn't like the idea of hiring a baby-sitter.

In Iran, its just what the elders do. They spend their time looking after every relative younger than them. Iranian parents never quit parenting. Our Grandmother Aziz is at the head of our family. She still keeps tabs on everyone. Only, now it's tough for her. The world has changed so much in her lifetime. She really can't keep track of some of her grandchildren when they're half a world away.

Sometimes I think it would be better for both my mother and grandmother to just let go. I think they should relax more and let their children take care of them for a change.

That was my feeling, but I guess my sister saw things differently. Within a few weeks, Mom arrived in Maryland to stay with Homa and Mohsen.

Our mother was in Iran when I married Robert and I had been reluctant to send her pictures of the wedding because she objected to my marrying an American.

After her first week in Bethesda, Homa made arrangements for our mother to fly out to Los Angeles so she could visit with my husband and me. She brought Homa's daughter with her.

That was a tough time for us. My mom took one look at my husband, Robert, and immediately decided I'd married the wrong man simply because he was not Iranian.

I'd already been married before, to an Iranian man, and that lasted only nine months. He didn't do a thing to make me feel that I should have a preference for men from the country of my birth. He, and

Mohsen, too, had similar traits. They seemed to believe women exist only so they can care for their men, and in return their men are supposed to take care of them and their brood.

The men bring home the money, to justify the arrangement, but what happens when the woman starts to work? You'd think the rules would change, but some people don't see it that way.

Our mother and I fought about this a lot. She couldn't get past my husband's fair skin and his blue eyes. "What in the world is wrong with Iranian men for you to choose an American?" she asked me several times, and I always responded the same way.

"Nothing, Mother, nothing. I just want someone around who sees me as a partner. Someone who can look in my eyes when I talk to him. Look at Dad. Has he ever looked into your eyes? Have you ever seen him look at you? And Mohsen is the same way. Do you ever see him listen when Homa talks? He never looks into her eyes when she talks, and she has a lot to say, like me. I just want someone to listen to me a little. My last husband couldn't do that either. He never listened. He only waited for his turn to speak. He'd have an opinion and he'd wait for me to finish talking so he could express it. But he wouldn't have any idea what I was saying. That's just how so many of them are. It's in the blood. I don't like it. Robert doesn't do that to me. He knows I have a lot to say. And he knows it means something."

Explaining this to Mother was like running straight into a wall. She wouldn't hear a bit of it. Mother made me understand that the inability to listen was a trait that really had little to do with the sex of the listener. I was complaining about Iranian men, but I might as well have been talking about her. Each time we'd have this conversation, she'd respond to one of my long-winded explanations about why I resent Iranian men, by saying something that could only mean she didn't hear a bit of what I'd said.

"You're Iranian, you are not American. It's not right for you to marry this way. Why did you do it?"

"Look, Mother. I met Robert and I liked him. We take good care of each other and that's all there is to it!"

But these conversations continued throughout her visit. She never took a liking to Robert. Because of that, she was cold toward him, and it made her stay nearly unbearable. The arguments made me feel as though I no longer had anything in common with my mother.

She refused to understand my feelings about men. Of course, this lack of comprehension was one of her worst personality traits. She could rarely empathize with anyone on an objective level.

At the time of her visit, Robert and I were both full-time students who worked our way through school as electronics technicians. We didn't have much money and what we did have usually went toward our expenses which included tuition, rent, and food, in that order. We rarely afforded all three. We were poor, in that respect.

But within days of her arrival, Mom wanted to know about the local nightclubs.

"When do you go out, I mean, to nightclubs? Don't you like to dance?"

"Well, Mom, we don't really have the time, or the money, or the energy for any of that." I told her.

"But this is America! Don't you guys go out all the time? Isn't that what it's all about?"

"Mom, who in the world gave you that idea?" All our mother knew about America came from movies she'd seen in Iran. She must have thought everyone here spent their lives at country clubs and played golf all day and danced all night. Her expectations were too high.

I wanted to give her a dose of reality. "Americans are people just like you and me. We are not in movies. This is life. We work, we go to school, and we sleep, and if it's a good day, we eat. I'm sorry, I wish I could offer you more. Believe me, one day I will. But right now I'm trying to build a life for myself. I'm starting from scratch here. I'll tell you, though, since the first day I came here, I've never wanted to go back. This is my home now. I like it here."

Our mother and Azita stayed with us for a very long month before returning to Bethesda.

Chapter 14

A Disastrous Christmas

After our mother came to Bethesda, our father decided he had no reason to remain in Iran. When Homa and Mohsen had their second daughter, Soraya, during the summer of 1969, he decided to come to America. At the time, Homa had finished her internship, and was fulfilling her residency requirement in pediatrics at the Freedmen's Hospital in Washington, D.C.

In order for our father to leave, he had to sell his business and use the cash to invest in real estate and buy a plane ticket. Of course, I was ecstatic when I heard he was coming. During that fall, Robert and I saved every penny we could in order to afford a trip to Bethesda that Christmas.

This was a historic trip for me. It solidified the negative feelings I was beginning to have about my relationship with the family. From the minute we arrived, Mohsen seemed disappointed to have us as houseguests.

In particular, he seemed uncomfortable with his American brother-in-law. But I did not know exactly what the problem was. On the day we arrived, the reception we received was cold and it set the tone for the rest of our visit.

It was as if our relationship was a microcosm of the larger world. Iran and the United States have been strange bedfellows over the latter half of the twentieth century. Political discussions about these two nations are guaranteed to be controversial under any circumstances.

Even so, Mohsen seemed overcome by the topic during our stay. He harped almost constantly on the United States government as if he were a soapbox orator. We might have ignored this, except that he insisted on using my husband as a target for all of his accusations.

He used any opportunity to corner Robert and demand an explanation for the United States' involvement in the Iranian coup d'état in 1953, when Prime Minister Mossadegh was stripped of his job for being a suspected Communist. He blamed this event on the strength of the CIA that supported it. He blamed the government for reinstating the shah. Mohsen likened the shah to a puppet whose strings were held by the president.

The topic was extremely sensitive and Mohsen's insistence on bringing it up aroused some difficult conversations, even between Robert and me.

We were getting ready for bed, after spending our first full day and night in Maryland, when my husband started asking me about Mohsen's attitude.

"Why is he acting so strange? I mean, I don't get it. He acts as though I have some control over foreign policy or something. He acts like I've done something to him. I've never met him! What is your sister doing with this guy?" Robert was very emotional when he said these things. He was angry, and his voice cracked while he spoke.

I didn't know what to say to him. I knew Mohsen was being ridiculous. He was really getting to Robert. My husband wasn't the type of a man who could walk away from a fight. He was very intelligent and he liked to debate things. But the arguments with Mohsen weren't debates at all. They were interrogations. Sometimes the tension in the room while they argued would grow so thick you could feel it.

I was embarrassed. I tried to downplay Mohsen's behavior. "Sweetheart, I understand that he's giving you a hard time, but I don't think he's trying to blame you for all the problems in Iran. He's just been frustrated by politics for a long time, and you are the first American he's had the chance to confront. It's his way of venting."

"None of that justifies what he's doing to me, or to our vacation."
"I know."

In order to avoid the constant conflicts at Homa's house, Robert and I tried to be there as little as possible. We started spending our days walking around Bethesda in their neighborhood. The walks were lovely, but it was hard for us because we did not have clothes to handle the weather. We lived in Los Angeles and the temperature never dropped below 40 degrees there. But in Bethesda in December, I'm not sure if the weather ever warmed up to 1 degree.

We were cold. We were also broke. Not having money or a car left us with little in the way of freedom to enjoy ourselves. It was shaping up to be a tough trip.

On our fourth day there, we had a major battle at the house and this pretty much severed any chance of Robert and Mohsen ever being close.

During the day, Robert and I had been out walking through the city. We found a vendor who'd been selling fresh live Maine lobsters. When the two of us saw those lobsters floating in the water tank, we couldn't resist the temptation. They are such a rare thing in California and the two of us could never afford such a meal back home. But on the street in Bethesda, they were inexpensive, and we were hungry and cold. We bought a few of them and brought them back to Homa's so we could all enjoy them for dinner.

On our way home, Robert and I were anxious and giddy. We walked through the neighborhood and talked about how much we were looking forward to our dinner. We really thought it was a good thing to do. We would make the dinner that night, and let our hosts rest for a while.

We were fools.

Sometimes you can get so excited about something, that you forget the kind of people you're surrounded by. My brother-in-law could not share our enthusiasm about the meal. He greeted us at the door and saw the boxes in our hand. He recognized what they were immediately.

Mohsen has a standard approach to greeting people that he uses every time he's introduced to someone. It's a methodical process that never changes, no matter who he's saying hello to. When he came to the door, he pulled it open to let us in and while he did this he started taking a deep breath so that his chest would inflate. You could say he did that to stand up straight and give the appearance that he was a gentleman, but it actually made you feel like he was trying to put distance between himself and you.

While holding his breath, he looked squarely at Robert, but he held his stare low and did not look in his eyes. They shook hands and then he turned to invite me in. While saying hello to me and asking me how my day was, he reached over and kissed me lightly on the cheek, but he did it in the same distant manner.

He doesn't look at you, he looks past you, as if he is really trying to find something that is behind you. This time, though, he had his eyes fixed on something else. While he kissed me, his attention didn't waver from the lobster boxes Robert was carrying.

"What is this? What did you bring back for us?"

"Oh, we found these downtown. They looked so good. We really couldn't resist. We thought dinner tonight could be a little different, and so we got these lobsters for everyone. Don't you think they'll be great?"

Mohsen didn't say anything. He wore a frozen grin on his face and his eyes looked a bit dazed.

"We can't get them out in California, not like these anyway. They cost a fortune out there." I was getting more excited just talking about them. "Here, honey, give them to me and I'll take them in the kitchen and start cooking."

And that was that. I went into the kitchen and Robert went to take a shower. Mohsen went to their bedroom.

About a half-hour later Homa came out from the bedroom to see me. She looked pale. I guessed she was a little upset.

"Parvin, what are you doing?" she asked.

"Tonight, Homa, Robert and I are going to make you dinner. We bought these lobsters, see? I'm getting everything else ready and he's going to be down soon to boil them. We planned it all out on the way home. Aren't you excited? This'll be the best meal we've been able to afford in years."

Homa started to speak agitatedly. Her voice had a high pitch.

"Why would you do that?" She spoke in a bitter tone. "What do you think? Have you forgotten that you're guests here?! Is something wrong with us? This is our home and we've cooked for you. Why would you want to change that? Do you know what you're saying to us by doing this?"

I was surprised by her attitude. I was almost shocked. "Now, Homa, you know that's not the case. We found this guy downtown selling the lobsters and we got excited about it. We're your guests, but I'm also your sister. We're family for goodness sake. I mean, we're all family. Robert and I wanted to do something for you before we left, and we thought this would be a good way to do it."

"Well, you are family—that's not the point. You're still guests in Maryland, and you're staying in our home. It's an insult you know. It's an insult to go and bring dinner home to your host. What's wrong with our food?! Don't you like Persian food anymore?"

Robert came in the kitchen and saw Homa and me arguing, but he couldn't understand what we were saying because we were speaking in Farsi. He was in the doorway of the kitchen and was looking to me for guidance. He wanted to know whether he should start cooking or just leave us alone for a while.

"Come on in, honey. The lobsters are over there on the counter. I think the water's already boiling. Don't worry about any of this."

He walked in and started opening the box to fetch the shellfish.

My sister and I continued sparing. "Homa, you know I like Persian food and Robert does, too. We love the food you've been preparing. We just saw the lobsters and got excited. We really didn't mean to insult you. Can't we just enjoy this one meal and leave this argument behind? I messed up. I made a mistake. What else can I say. At this point there's nothing I can do." I couldn't understand my sister's objections, but I was tired of arguing. I just wanted to eat and get it over with. It was beginning to seem like Homa and I were fighting over anything and everything.

"Well, what you've done is wrong!" With that, my sister turned and left the kitchen. She returned to their bedroom, and I turned toward Robert to help him with the food.

I went over to the counter and started preparing some vegetables for a side dish. I was washing some pea pods and all I was thinking about was the argument I had just had with Homa.

In all my life, I'd never seen her so easily insulted. She acted as if we had really hurt her feelings by bringing a few lobsters home. Still, I believe the feelings weren't genuine. They didn't seem to be when she expressed them.

It must have come from her husband. After he let us in, he went to their bedroom. He must have told Homa about the lobsters. They probably fought about it for awhile before she came out to talk to me.

Mohsen, himself, was just stubborn when it came to food, I think. He refused to eat anything that wasn't Iranian. He wouldn't think of having a meal created by any other culture. In his view, we'd insulted our hosts by bringing the lobsters because that meant we were indirectly hinting that we disapproved of the food normally served in his home.

Homa came back to get something to drink. When she did, we spoke again.

"It's him, isn't it?" I wanted to confront her and show her how her husband was controlling her thoughts.

She pulled me aside so that Robert couldn't hear what we were saying. "Look, I don't really care that you brought the lobsters, but Mohsen has a point. It wasn't a very considerate thing to do. I mean, you know how he feels about America. He doesn't like the country or its food. Why, then, would you purposely upset him this way?"

Her words made me wonder how she could possibly be related to me. "If he hates it here so much, what the hell is he doing in this country? Why not just go back to Iran?"

"He's only here to complete his residency and then he'll go back."

"What? You guys are going back?"

"He is. I haven't decided what I'm going to do yet."

Homa and I then set the table and our mother served the Iranian dishes she had prepared. I placed the lobsters on the table with some melted butter. I hoped that we could all make it through dinner without anymore arguing, but I knew that was probably an impossibility.

In fact, almost the minute we sat down to eat, a heated discussion broke out between Mohsen and Robert. The debate consisted of a constant barrage of questions being thrown at Robert by his brother-in-law. Finally, Robert, almost totally humiliated, asked Mohsen why he was in the United States if he hated the country so much.

"America is feeding on the blood of the innocent people all over the world, including my country!" Mohsen said.

Robert replied. "How is America feeding on the blood of your people?"

"They're taking our oil and supporting the shah so he can murder the citizens of our country. You know, it's the American corporations that benefit from selling their filthy Western products in Iran. The United States is becoming more and more wealthy at the expense of poor Iranians!" This is how Mohsen argued. He flew from issue to issue in a very disorderly fashion. One could almost call it ranting.

Homa interrupted her husband. "Honey, Robert had nothing to do with what happened in Iran. You have to understand that! Stop it now, he's my sister's husband and they are our guests and we should respect that. Come on now, stop discussing politics!"

"How can you say it is not his fault?! He votes for his representatives! Their government does what its people ask it to do. They started the Savak in Iran so they could kill as many people as they wanted. On the day of the coup d'état in 1953, I was there in the bazaar. I saw it with my own eyes. They were passing out vodka and U.S. dollar bills to the drunks downtown and telling them to beat the students and loot businesses. They manufactured the uprising that removed Mossadegh!" He pointed at Robert. "His country! They are imperialists and they have no mercy for people like ours." Mohsen continued his assault. He was filled with energy because he had finally found an American to bitch at for all of his country's problems.

Robert stood up, tossed his napkin on the table, and looked toward Moshen. "Ah, hell! To hell with it. If you don't like living in freedom, just go back to your dictatorial country and live in fear of your government forever! You think you have it so good back there. Well listen, I'm not here to defend America's leadership, but there's a reason this country became as powerful as it is! Why the hell don't you just get the hell out of here? You weren't invited. You can just leave."

Robert started to get truly emotional. He continued screaming at Mohsen.

"You wouldn't leave, though, would you? You're here for a reason and you know it. You're here to get something you'd never be able to get in Iran! It's our freedom that made all that possible. You're nothing but a leech in these United States, and you disgust me. I've no idea what a woman as lovely as your wife is doing with someone like your-self. I really wonder."

Robert turned to me then, and asked me to come with him. He wanted to leave their home, right then and there. But it was too late for us to leave. We didn't have enough money to catch a cab or get a hotel room.

I went outside with my husband for a little while. Once we both calmed down, I brought him back to our room. The next morning, we made new plans as soon as we woke up. My sister took us both to the bus station. We boarded a bus going to Vermont. Robert had a brother there.

It was the first time I'd been in my sister's home, and we only lasted four days.

Chapter 15

Seeds of Separation

During the next three years, Homa and I communicated only by phone, usually once every week. By August 1970, Homa had completed her first year of residency in pediatrics. At the time, Mohsen had been working toward his residency in psychiatry. He decided he didn't want to continue in that specialty, and so he switched.

Switching meant he needed to start residency over again, and that put Homa ahead to become a licensed doctor one year before him. This disparity caused some problems for both of them. Homa told me they were arguing and the marriage was strained. She decided to quit working for one year so that Mohsen could catch up with her.

The year she stayed home was a difficult one for Homa. She didn't like not having any place to report to in the morning. She was convinced, however, that it was best for the family. She had two young girls to look after, and her thirst for politics kept her occupied.

Homa paid close attention to the human-rights violations that were going on in Iran at the time. She worked with different political parties. She produced her own flyers to raise awareness to the fact that people in Iran were not being permitted to speak against the government or to peacefully assemble to criticize the status quo.

Finally, in July 1971, Homa started working again. By then, she and Mohsen had moved to New Jersey. Homa started her second year of residency in pediatrics at the Misericordia-Fordham Hospital in New York.

Homa's one-year sabbatical from her studies had not achieved the effect she hoped for. She and Mohsen were still having difficulty. I knew their marriage was in jeopardy.

In 1972 I was working in Glendale, California. I was also enrolled in the University of Southern California (USC), trying to earn a master's degree in engineering. Robert was a graduate of the School of Journalism and was working for a trade publishing company.

By now my sister had finished her internship in Bethesda and was a practicing pediatrician in New York. She was still living with Mohsen and our father, but our mother had returned to Iran.

She left very soon after our father's arrival in Bethesda. She was separated from him for about a year after she came to my sister's home and before he was able to sell his business and move to America. I guess the time apart allowed each of them to become comfortable with the idea of being alone.

Our father enjoyed being free from his wife. He enjoyed exploring the country on his own. His wife, on the other hand, was disappointed with the United States. She never adjusted to the fact that life here just wasn't glamorous.

In Iran, she could tolerate her husband, but here, divorce was all she talked about. Homa and I knew that the two of them needed to be separated. Father decided to stay with Homa and there was nothing for our mother to do but return to Tehran.

By the time July came around, I had discovered that I was pregnant. I still went to school in the evening and worked most days, but every once in a while I had to stay home because I was too sick to work.

It was a hot Saturday morning. I had a bad case of morning sickness. Around 10 A.M., I went outside to sit in the shade in our yard. We had a nice backyard that we used mostly as a garden for vegetables and strawberries. We also had some chairs and a table there that we liked to use during the warmer months for dining.

I was sitting in one of the chairs with my eyes closed and a damp washcloth on my forehead. I was thinking about growing up in Tehran and wondering how I ever survived the heat. The phone rang and I went inside to answer it.

"Hi, Parvin. It is me, Homa." I hadn't spoken with my sister for almost a month.

"Homa, how are you?"

"I'm okay." There was tension in her voice.

"Is something wrong? You don't sound so good," I asked.

"Oh, Parvin, I'm just fed up with my life right now. I can't stand living with my husband anymore. He never helps me with anything. I'm the one responsible for seeing that the children are taken care of and making sure enough food is in the house. He doesn't lift a finger. I'm tired of it. I don't want a divorce, because I don't want our daughters to suffer. But I don't know what to do or how to get away from him.

"I really want to find a way out. I want to leave, and I want to take my children with me, but I just don't know how."

"Are you sure?"

"Of course!"

"Then you'll need plane tickets. How much money do you have?"

"But that's just it, I don't know. Mohsen keeps a tight leash on me. I don't know where my money goes, or where our bank account is. I give my paycheck to him and he pays the bills. And when he's done with those, he gives me an allowance for the week."

"Jesus! Homa, I thought things weren't so great between the two of you, but I never thought it was this bad."

"Oh, Parvin, I don't know who else to call. Please help me."

"Of course. I'll start right away."

The next day I called the School of Medicine at USC. I also called UCLA to see if they had any openings.

After a few days of calling the medical centers, I finally had some answers for my sister. I called her a week after her original call. It was Saturday again.

"I've got good news for you, Homa. USC and UCLA are both willing to hire you. You need to complete one more year in an internship position because California requires a two-year internship, but they will accept your accrued time at Bethesda. They can offer you $25,000 that year and if you want to earn more money, you can spend some of your nights in the emergency room."

Homa's response was not as enthusiastic as I would have thought. "Thank you, Parvin, but I'm not sure. One more year of interning might place too heavy a burden on Father and the children. Dad hasn't been too happy lately and I'm afraid he'll become severely depressed if I continue working such long hours. I just don't think I can do this to him."

I felt she was making excuses. "But Homa, if you come out here and get a place close to us, I can watch over Father and take care of your children while you work. You know, I'm pregnant now and so Dad can have fun with the newborn. You know how much he loves to sit and watch babies. He should be fine out here."

"Well, I have to think more. Give me some time."

Homa didn't move to California. She didn't like the idea of having to spend an entire year working as an intern again. She was also being pressured by our mother to stay with Mohsen.

At the end of the year she completed her residency in pediatrics and started a new one in child psychiatry at the Harlem Hospital Center which was associated with Columbia University. For the next two years, she worked toward that requirement.

Once our mother returned to Iran, she figured out that she liked it better in the United States. She came back to be with Robert and me in January 1973, so she could be here when I gave birth. By then, we'd bought a two-bedroom home in Atwater, California, a small city very close to Dodger Stadium in Los Angeles.

Our son, Romin, was born at 9 P.M. on February 12. Within five weeks, I was working full-time again and our mother was looking after Romin. But she felt uncomfortable living with us so she found a place where she could be alone.

I agreed to cover her expenses for an apartment as long as she would ride the bus to our place every morning and watch Romin. At night, I would take her back home in my car.

We had a smooth arrangement, and it worked for nearly a month.

Eventually, however, Mother came to me and said she had to leave for New Jersey. She said Homa needed her help.

"But, Mom, what about me? Look at all the work I've done to set you up with an apartment. This wasn't easy, you know. Besides, I really need your help with Romin. Why do you want to go?"

"Parvin, I have no choice! Homa called and said that your father is going back to Iran and she needs someone to take care of her daughters. Just cancel the lease on the apartment. You can handle it. I know you can. Your sister needs me. She's not the same as you."

And that was that. The next day I took her to the airport and she flew to New Jersey. I wasn't really surprised by her decision to leave. She has always been an unhappy person and she usually doesn't like to stay in one place very long. She blames her environment for her depression. For that reason, I had rented the apartment on a month-to-month basis. I was penalized only one month's rent when she moved.

Interestingly, our father did not leave for Iran right away. Homa had asked for Mother because he was becoming sick. He was struggling with the workload demanded at their home.

With his distaste of foreign foods, Mohsen refused to eat at restaurants. He never ordered food for delivery, and he wouldn't bring anything home when he came from work. Instead, the burden of preparing meals was on his in-laws.

Iranian food, however, is very time-consuming to prepare, and since it was the only thing Mohsen would permit, Mom and Dad had to spend most of their days preparing the vegetables and other ingredients for traditional Persian meals.

So while they both lived there, they spent almost all of their time working for Homa and her husband. Mohsen would come from work and sit in his chair and call on one of them to bring him tea. They cooked, cleaned, raised the children, and took care of all the chores.

But living together still overwhelmed our parents. After a few months they went through official divorce proceedings. Mother left for Iran, for the second time, to get an official Islamic divorce and a financial settlement. Their marriage ended after thirty-six years and the split caused problems for each of them.

Upon her return to Iran, our mother became more depressed than ever. Father lost his home to her through the divorce settlement. At the age of sixty-nine, our father, who had worked and lived independently since he was twelve years old, was forced to live with his daughter and son-in-law in New Jersey.

It was a Sunday morning in 1974, and I was getting breakfast ready when Homa called from New Jersey.

"Parvin! You have to come out here! You have to come right away if you want to see our father again. It doesn't look like he'll make it much longer." She was panicking and she spoke so fast that it was hard to understand her.

"Homa, what are you talking about? What's going on? What's wrong with Dad?"

"His appendix has ruptured. We put him through one operation, but he needs another one. We don't think he can survive a second operation, though. You have to come."

"When? When did this happen?" I hadn't heard a word about our father for weeks.

"We just noticed it. We don't know when it happened."

"But you're both doctors! How could you not notice when the man's appendix ruptures?!"

"You know how he is. He had a stomach ache for a couple of days, but he never said anything. I saw him the other night and his skin was pale. I gave him an examination and rushed him to the hospital immediately.

"You know, because he was a heavy drinker for most of his life, he's developed an enlarged liver. To add to that, he has high blood pressure and cholesterol levels.

"He's lucky, though, because he's surrounded by doctors. Because of us, Dad's in good hands, but I am so worried. Please, if you want to see him for the last time, you better be here tomorrow morning before he goes in for the next operation."

I got off the phone and booked a red-eye flight to New York. By seven the next morning I arrived in New York with my son. Mohsen was there to pick us up. After stopping to leave Romin at home with Homa and her daughters, we went straight to the hospital.

I entered the intensive-care unit where our father was lying sick. His skin was pale. It looked as though he hadn't been outside for months. He seemed slender and weak. Seeing my dad in such a condition made me sad.

I held his hand and spoke to him, hesitantly. "Dad. How are you?" A stupid question, I guess. "It's me, Parvin."

I don't understand what happened after I greeted him, but he opened his eyes wide and looked at me as if he was amazed. He asked me about Romin and my husband. Then he asked me what I was doing in the hospital.

"I was worried about you," I said.

That statement triggered something within the old man. It was as if the color came back to his face instantly. He looked over at me and the two of us spent the next hour or so talking. Before long, we were laughing and arguing, completely ignoring our surroundings. Then, in walked one of his doctors.

I felt my heart fall to the floor. He'd come to prepare my father for the operation that was to take place. But whatever brought my dad back to life, the doctor noticed, too. He took a look at a few of the machines in the room and decided to delay the operation.

I'll never forget his words: "He's improved." The doctor spoke in a normal tone, as if he wasn't surprised at all. "We'll give it some more time." And then he left.

Later, we brought Romin to the hospital and he got to spend some time with his grandfather. As the hours passed, we watched him become more vibrant and stronger. That evening, his doctor decided to cancel the operation.

"Mr. Darabi," he said, "just needed a little attention from his younger daughter. Seeing her is all he needed to get well." It was an odd diagnosis, but there seemed to be little else to explain the improvement. That day I learned the value of a little affection.

Mohsen, though, was as bitter as ever. The explanation didn't sit well with him at all. He insisted that his colleague must have made an error in his initial diagnosis. He might have been right, I guess. I just didn't think it mattered. I only cared to hear that my dad wasn't so sick anymore.

He was moved to the regular ward. I stayed with him for the next two days. Once I was assured that he was out of danger, I left with my son for Los Angeles. The three days in Mohsen's house were more than enough after my last visit.

The news from our father did not stay positive. Within a year, he was diagnosed with prostate cancer. We knew he wouldn't live long, but Homa did her best to care for him.

Chapter 16

On Her Own

A surprising turn of events in my sister's life occurred later that year. Mohsen went back to Iran, for good. Homa was left with our father and her two daughters. I was surprised by Mohsen's decision to leave, and I asked Homa about it.

"Why does he want to live in Iran? With both of you being doctors you can have a great life here."

"You know Mohsen. He likes to be in Iran. Here, he is just another doctor. America is saturated with them. In Iran, though, they are God-like. No one questions their judgments and they are treated like royalty. He likes the feeling."

"But what about you? Doesn't he want to be with you?"

"I don't know. We haven't been getting along lately. We don't have much of a life together. The important thing is that this is temporary. Our daughters shouldn't be hurt. I'm trying to get a residency in general psychiatry. I still have some time to put in. Once I finish, I'll have to decide what to do about our marriage."

Homa finished her residency in child psychiatry in June 1974 and began her third specialty in September 1974 at the Metropolitan Hospital Center which was associated with the New York Medical College.

I knew, of course, that Homa and her husband were having trouble, but the news that he had left still came as a shock. "I can't believe he just left without you."

"Well, back home it's common for a husband to live apart from his wife and children, you know that. I think it's the right time for me to live alone for a while."

"I just hope you guys don't end up going through what Mom and Dad did when they were separated."

"I don't think we will. It should be a good thing for us."

I kept in touch with Homa a lot in the weeks that followed. It seemed to take her a while to adjust to being alone. Once she did, though, her approach to life seemed to change dramatically. It was the first time she ever learned to live on her own. She was an extremely busy woman in those days. In October 1974 she received her license to practice medicine and surgery in the state of New Jersey. That effectively allowed her to practice in any state except New York, Florida, and California. Still, she didn't open a private practice. Instead, she continued working toward her residency in general psychiatry.

We spoke by phone almost every week. Our relationship hadn't been as close since we were children in Iran.

"So, how are things?"

"Fine, Parvin, fine. I am adjusting well. I've got my own home, my own bank account, and my own car. It's a lot of responsibility."

"I know, but it sounds like you're handling things well. How about the children, how are they?" I asked.

"I think they're fine. The school is very close and I let them walk every day. You know, Dad's great also. He runs around during the day and manages to do all the cooking. On Saturdays, we all get together and do the shopping for the rest of the week. That leaves us Sundays to go sightseeing or visit friends or entertain. I have to say, things are really working out."

"What do you think, then. Are you going to leave? Mom wants you to go back to Mohsen."

"I know she does. I would like to return to Iran but I don't think I can leave right now. I'd like to try and stay in America. I've even petitioned for citizenship, and it looks like I'll get it within a few months."

"Wow. That would be great. Why don't you try and license yourself to practice out here in California? That way we can be closer. It's easier for you, because you're a doctor. That gives you a lot of flexibility."

"Well, It's going to take me two years to complete my work in general psychiatry and then I can think about California."

These conversations were pleasant. We avoided politics and tried not to mother each other. It was a working formula. It did a lot to further our friendship as adults.

In April 1975, I received an offer from the Iranian Electronics Industry to work in Iran for one year. I asked Homa what she thought about the idea of me going back.

She loved it. "Parvin, I think you should. Iran is our home. We were raised there and we should respect that. Also, they need us. They have a brain-drain problem over there. Skilled people like you and I are a dime-a-dozen in this country, but there are so few back home. I think it's important that we try to help as much as we can." She spoke with strong conviction.

I wasn't sure though.

"I don't know. I'm not sure I can handle it. Robert wants to go. He remembers our vacation there last year. He fell in love with the family and the country. I think he really wants to live in Iran for a while. Still, I just don't like dealing with the gender segregation, even with the Family Protection Act. I don't really want to raise our son in that environment."

"But Romin can go to an American school because his father's American. Just try, and if you don't like it, you can always find another job in California."

I knew why Homa felt so strongly about returning. She loved Iran. She missed it all the time. I think she only stayed in the United States because she felt it was best for her daughters and her career. The dream of returning never left her. She had always wanted to go back and use her education to help the people there. Deep down, I knew that one day she would.

I spent the next couple of months thinking hard about whether leaving was going to be a good idea. In June 1975, Homa became licensed to practice in New York, but she was still trying to complete her residency in general psychiatry.

I ended up accepting the job in Iran. I left for Tehran in the first week of July 1975. I took Romin with me, but Robert stayed behind because I wasn't certain the move would be permanent.

My colleagues at work gave me eight weeks. They said I'd be fed up with Iran in eight weeks and I'd come home by then.

They were wrong. It took seven.

For the trip back to the United States, I arranged my flight so Romin and I could spend a day in New York with Homa. It didn't work out, though, because our mother got involved in the planning.

She wouldn't let me call Homa from Iran because she thought it would be too expensive. Instead, I had to call her from the airport as I passed through customs. When I did she wasn't home. I changed our flight and went straight back to Los Angeles. I called Homa and found out what went wrong.

"Homa? It's me, I'm back."

"I know, I heard. Mom told me you were returning. But why weren't you at the airport today? We waited for hours by one of the doors."

"I don't understand, why were you there?" I asked.

"Mother told us you were staying over. She told us to go get you."

I couldn't believe what I was hearing. "She told me to call you once I got to the airport! She didn't want to spend the money for the long-distance call."

"Oh, I can't believe it."

"I called your home over and over again, but no one answered, so I gave up. I had to come home."

"The whole time you were calling, we were outside the customs area, waiting."

"But JFK has a few customs doors. How did you know at which one to wait?"

"We didn't." The answer was obvious. "I guess we picked the wrong one."

"Sometimes I just can't understand Mother." I was frustrated and annoyed because I really wanted to stay with Homa for a while.

"That's just the way she is," she said. "I'm sorry we missed you."

Romin and I needed to rest, so I ended the phone call. Homa called back a week later.

"I started my new job today," I told her, "It's a company close by. I called them the day after I arrived and they interviewed me the following day. Now we have a little income to get by on." My husband had to quit his job. "He's a little disappointed because I wouldn't stay in Iran. I try to make him understand the problems back home."

"Was it bad?"

"Money from the oil has introduced rapid growth. The population seems to be exploding faster than the infrastructure can handle. Housing is short. Food is expensive and the pollution is terrible. It's not the country in which we grew up."

"What about the work. How was that?"

"It was tough. I couldn't work freely. The head of the company told me I was to work with Americans. He said I wouldn't be allowed to train any Iranians."

"That's ridiculous! Did you object?"

"I told him I was working in America with Americans. I explained that I wanted to help some of the local professionals by developing some of their skills."

"Good. What did he say to that?"

"Nothing! Can you believe it?! He asked me to leave. He excused me from his presence and that was it."

"Oh my, what an experience." Homa sounded very disappointed. I think she really wanted me to find a way to live in Iran. "What else?" she asked.

"During my final week, a memo came around demanding that all employees start reporting at five in the evening each day to rehearse the national anthem. They wanted us to be ready to sing for the shah if he ever came by.

"I just don't have the patience for these kinds of things. But those weren't the key problems. I never realized the hidden agendas that surrounded my projects. Politics were omnipresent in the company and my reports started to cause trouble because I wouldn't support the status quo, which was shut up and bend with the wind.

"I had to leave."

"Well, it sounds like you made the right decision. It's depressing, though, because I really miss Iran. In America, I feel like a foreigner."

"I don't know. I can't feel too homesick for a country that treats people like that one does."

"The people aren't the problem," Homa said.

"I know."

"I just miss it," she continued. "It was our home. I still owe that country, too. You can't forget that I have a degree because people there paid for it. Sometimes I feel bad for leaving."

Chapter 17

Democracy Will Replace the Monarchy

Nineteen seventy-six was a difficult year for me. Robert and I had separated and were struggling through a divorce procedure. I'd just purchased a home in Orange County for my son and me.

Homa was still living in New Jersey and she had completed her third residency.

"Homa? It's Parvin. I'm sorry to wake you like this but Romin and I are very sick, and we can't sleep."

I could hear my sister on the other end of the line, fumbling the receiver. "What's wrong?" she said in a slurred voice. "Tell me the symptoms."

"We have high temperatures, clogged noses, and it's difficult to breathe. Neither one of us has slept at all tonight and Romin won't stop crying."

"Do you have a vaporizer at home?" Homa asked.

"Yes."

"Okay, here's what you have to do." Suddenly Homa spoke in a clear voice. She sounded as if I was calling her at noon. "Fill the vaporizer with water and place it in the center of your bed, pull a sheet over the two of you, and try to sleep. Call me in the morning when you wake up."

Her suggestion worked. We slept straight through the night.

I didn't wake up until the phone rang the following day, at two in the afternoon.

"Hello?"

"Parvin? Is that you? Are you still sleeping?"

"No," I replied, but my speech was broken. "What time is it?"

"I waited a while for you to call this morning. I was worried."

"I guess we slept through most of the day. Your idea worked, though. I feel fine today. I guess I better get up."

"Don't do that. Have some juice and take a couple of aspirin with Romin and go back to sleep. The more you rest, the better off you'll be. If your fever continues, see a doctor. I'll call you back later."

Homa was always available to help when it came to these kinds of things. Day or night. This time it was 5 A.M. when I called her. I was desperate. It was a comfort knowing she was a doctor I could call on at any time.

Nineteen seventy-six was also a tough year for Homa. She was having doubts about her decision to stay in the United States. She'd been separated from her husband for a long time, and they both might have felt as if they were losing each other. Homa was getting used to living alone, but she might have worried about losing the chance to ever reconcile with Mohsen. When she completed her residency, it gave her an excuse to return to Iran.

By that time, Homa had become an American citizen, but I don't think she ever convinced herself that she would stay in America permanently. She loved Iran. She also felt like she had abandoned it. She knew Iran needed doctors more than America did.

Mother was convinced that her daughter was making a mistake by leaving Mohsen for so long. She thought it would harm the children. She also knew that Mohsen had the power to take the girls away from Homa if the three of them came back to Iran. That was Iranian law.

Indeed, to stay in the United States, Homa would have to convince herself that she might never be able to return to Iran. That would have been too great a sacrifice.

But it was Mohsen who actually got her to return. He came to the United States in the latter part of 1976 and pushed for the two of them to live together again.

Once back in Iran, Homa started teaching psychiatry at the School of Medicine at the University of Tehran. The university was affiliated with a hospital and she worked there also. But with her free time, she opened her own practice. To be a professor in Iran is an extremely prestigious accomplishment. She was proud of her new job because it was exactly what she dreamed of doing for the country. She wanted to help the future of Iran by developing young minds.

As her private practice grew, she quickly established an excellent reputation across the country. Doctors from every part of Iran referred patients to see her in Tehran. She enjoyed her practice, but it was obvious that her real pleasure came in teaching. I really believe that accepting that job was, in her mind, the pinnacle of her career.

For two years, we were forced to speak by phone because I wouldn't find the time to travel to Iran. In 1978, however, I saw my sister in California.

I was living in Northern California. Homa, Mohsen, and their daughters came to the United States to visit family and Homa wanted to earn two more certifications. While on the trip, she took the exam to enter the American Board of Psychiatry and Neurology. She was nervous about that test because no Iranian had ever passed it before.

During the summer, the family came out to California to see me. While in the state, Homa took a written exam to get licensed in California.

Then they moved on to Ohio to visit some of Mohsen's siblings that lived there. When the rest of the family returned to Iran, Homa came back to California. She needed to take the oral portion of California's exam.

Homa was still struggling with the question of where she wanted to live. Like most decisions she faced, she was having difficulty making this one. Apparently, she wanted to be licensed in California so that she would always have the option of living there if she ever left Iran.

Mohsen had told her not to bother with the American Board of

Psychiatry exam. He thought she wouldn't pass because it was known to be a difficult test. I guess they fought about it, and Mohsen let her take it because he was convinced she'd fail.

She didn't.

In November 1978 my sister became the first Iranian ever to become a member of the American Board of Psychiatry and Neurology. It was a proud moment for our entire family.

One evening during her stay with me, I invited a few of my Iranian colleagues along with their families to enjoy a nice dinner and to meet my sister. Our mother was living with me at the time.

These are the kinds of occasions that usually work fine, so long as no one wants to discuss politics or religion. It was inevitable, however, that someone would open such a discussion. In Iran, at the time, the Ayatollah Khomeini was trying to mount an overthrow of the shah. He was in Paris, and the foreign media were helping him by keeping him prominently featured in the news.

Homa was still the activist she'd been when she was young. "Start selling everything you own, and come back to Iran," she told us all. We were in the living room relaxing after our meal with a few bottles of wine. "A revolution has started and within a few months we will be free of the shah." Homa continued, "Democracy will replace the monarchy and Iran will be a free nation for the first time in its history."

"But, Homa," I said, "Khomeini is a religious man. Don't you know that religion and politics don't mix?"

"You just don't understand!" She was emphatic. She spoke to everyone. "You're here in your luxurious homes in America. You've all forgotten what's going on in Iran.

"Khomeini is an intelligent, educated man. He has been trained in Russia. He's written several books. He wants to free Iran from the atrocities of the shah and give the country to the people. He has no desire to be a politician or to rule the country."

Homa the activist was a challenge to argue with. "What books?!" I asked. "They've all been burned. The shah exiled Khomeini in 1963, and he had all the books destroyed."

One of the guests spoke up. "Homa, what is wrong with the shah?"

"Are you kidding?" she replied. "He has bottled the blood of Iranians to feed his greed."

We were all looking at Homa, confused.

"He is taking money from Iran and placing it in Swiss bank accounts for himself. He's selling out our future. The debt this year is $7.4 billion.

"Do you remember in 1971, when he gave the most ostentatious party in the history of mankind in order to celebrate twenty-five hundred years of monarchy in Persia? Two hundred million dollars were spent in foreign countries for that event while Iranian people were starving to death from malnutrition. Presidents, princes, and dignitaries from sixty-nine nations feasted on caviar and roast peacocks catered by companies in Paris.

"They drank French wine out of Baccarat crystal, and while Iran grows the most beautiful flowers in the world, flowers for this event were imported from Denmark. Now how can you tolerate this from the leader of a small, poor country like Iran?"

"But he wanted to celebrate a major event in our history," said another guest.

"What event? Iran never had 2,500 years of continuous monarchy. We know that the first king, Kouroush Kabir, was crowned in 559 B.C.E. To get to 1971, would take 2,530 years. Second, Iran exchanged its monarchy for a constitutional monarchy in 1906 when Mozaferaldin Shah signed the Constitution into law."

"No. I don't buy it. It was a party and that's all," said the guest.

"So, he gave a party and he spent too much. Is that so wrong?" The first guest joined in again.

"Do you think we are condemning him for a party and nothing else? What about the crimes of the Savak? What about all the people who've been tortured and killed in his prisons?"

"They're usually Communists."

"Even a Communist has rights." This was an unpopular attitude, even in America. I think she may have recognized that and changed her line of argument. "In 1964, in exchange for two hundred million dollars from the United States, the shah passed a bill that gave American military personnel immunity from any crimes they committed in

Iran. This is outrageous!" Homa was beginning to become visibly angry.

She was leaning forward in her chair and using her hands dramatically. "At the time, Khomeini said the shah had reduced Iranian citizens to a level lower than that of an American dog: 'If someone runs over such a dog,' he said, 'he would have to be prosecuted. If an American soldier rapes and shoots an Iranian woman, however, no one could do anything.' He was right!"

I immediately remembered what Homa was talking about. She had written to me in 1964. She had sent me an article describing the bill. Homa told me then that she distrusted the United States and the shah. She said she wouldn't stop fighting until the law was overturned.

After I read the article, I had similar feelings about the bill. It seemed as though the entire governing body of Iran was a servant of American diplomacy.

I sympathized with the Iranian people. Like Homa, I believed in change, but I couldn't support the *mullahs*. I thought of our father's convictions and refused to support Khomeini.

The discussion was quickly turning into an argument. I had to do something to prevent a fight. I interrupted everyone and asked the guests to make a pledge with me.

"We don't believe in the law of the clergy. Therefore, we will not return to Iran at this time. But if Khomeini establishes a democracy, independent of religion, we can all make our own effort to help rebuild the country."

Everyone agreed to that.

"For now, we should enjoy some of the delicious desserts our mother has prepared. She worked all day on our meal."

The rest of the night went smoothly as the conversation turned to more subtle topics.

A few days later, Homa returned to Ohio and then to Iran. She was needed back at the university. She had big plans for Iran.

One of Homa's deep regrets about Iran stemmed from the manner in which the nation traditionally dealt with problem children. Children suffering from mental disorders like hyperactivity, schizophrenia, depression, or attention disorder were considered insane and were committed to state-owned mental institutions which were little more than prisons. The government doctors did not know what else to do with them. These children were considered untreatable.

Homa had spent several years qualifying herself in the United States so she could one day return to Iran to establish a clinic where children with these disorders could be treated. Upon her return, she did just that.

Establishing the clinic was a challenge for Homa, but finding patients was not. Children were brought from all over the country to be treated by her. These were children that were destined to be nothing more than inmates in state hospitals. She was changing their lives for the better.

The job gave her tremendous satisfaction.

Chapter 18

A Black Day for Iran

On the morning of November 4, 1979, while I was on a trip in Austria, I was enjoying a breakfast of various breads, cheeses, cold cuts, and jams. There were a few others eating at the tables around me and the restaurant was half full. The ceiling had small speakers embedded in it, and I could hear the radio in the background while I ate.

There was a man's voice on the radio and he was speaking quickly in rather short sentences. I could not understand the language, so I had to listen for proper nouns. I tried to guess the news by connecting the proper names that came together in sentences.

Iran and the *United States*.

This combination started coming up repeatedly for about five minutes of the broadcast. I still understood nothing, but the speaker's tone worried me. I knew something terrible must have occurred.

By this time, Khomeini had returned to Iran and taken over leadership of the country. The shah had fled, unable to compete with the immense popularity of his rival. Indeed, Khomeini had manipulated the power of the media perfectly during his exile in France.

Before my trip, the shah had come to the United States to get medical assistance. I knew this would anger people in Iran. Many now saw

159

their former monarch as an enemy. Any country that accepted him would also have to be considered an enemy. Before I left for Europe, I feared for any Americans left in Iran.

Now, as I drank my morning coffee, I started to fear the worst.

It was Sunday, and my next meeting was scheduled for Monday in Bonn, West Germany. After breakfast, I picked up my bags and drove to Bonn. On my way, I tried to find an English-speaking station on the radio, but I couldn't. I just kept hearing the same two proper names over and over again on the German radio. When I finally arrived in Cologne, I called Homa in Tehran.

"Homa? What's going on over there? It sounds like something awful is happening."

"Oh, God! Parvin! Where are you? It's terrible! It's November fourth, today. The anniversary of Khomeini's exile in 1964. It was also the first anniversary of a bloody clash that erupted between the shah's national guards and some students at the University of Tehran. Anyway, I guess emotions were high." She sounded upset as she talked.

"In the morning, a group of women with black *chadors* came through the front gate of the U.S. embassy and started demonstrating. You know, they blamed the United States for supporting the shah during his monarchy.

"Then a huge group of men—students from the university— stormed into the embassy shouting 'Death to America!' They started grabbing the Americans and taking them as hostages.

"They blindfolded their prisoners and some of them even held pistols to their captives' heads while parading them in front of television cameras." She had to stop for a while because she was crying.

I couldn't believe what I was hearing. My heart sank as I thought of the ramifications of what was happening. I suddenly understood the urgent tone with which the local radio was presenting the news.

Homa started talking again. "This is awful! We never wanted this! Parvin? Where are you now? You have to be careful!"

"Don't worry about me. I'm in West Germany now. But I can't believe this is happening. I wonder why the United States government didn't foresee it. They could have protected the Americans in the embassy."

"I wonder, too," Homa said. "It seems like the Americans had a lot to do with Khomeini's rise. I think the shah was getting too strong for them and driving the price of gasoline too high. They might have wanted to get rid of him, but they replaced him with the wrong guy."

"But, Homa, the Iranian people supported him. I read that 98 percent of eligible voters voted the Islamic Republic into power."

"Only because he fooled the nation. He was brought in as a *mohallel* [a *mohallel* is a man who mediates between a previously divorced couple that want to remarry] to bring democracy to Iran and then leave for Gom [a city in Iran where the religious hierarchy reside] and preach his religion."

Khomeini made this promise, but once he gained control of the government, he had a change of heart and decided to hold a vote so people could decide whether they wanted the government to adopt his interpretation of the Islamic religion and established an Islamic republic.

"The vote wasn't fair, though," she continued. "People were told that if they supported the Islamic Republic, they'd receive free water and electricity and the government would deliver kerosene to their homes free of charge. Khomeini even promised free housing to all families with six or more children."

"And people actually believed they could have all these things for free?" I said, not understanding why the populace would be so naive.

"They didn't know better. And Khomeini convinced them that the oil revenues would be sufficient to supply everyone with a comfortable living."

"But it's not possible. There are thirty-five million people in Iran."

"They don't understand, Parvin."

"It's awful."

"I never expected this."

"I know, Homa."

When I got off the phone, I sat alone in my hotel room and thought about our conversation. Homa might have been correct in comparing Khomeini to a *mohallel*.

Under Islam, a man can divorce his wife simply by announcing his intention three times. After the third statement, the divorce is final.

Often, though, a married couple would have a heated argument and the husband would announce his intention to divorce his spouse in the heat of passion. Then, as soon as he cooled off, he might regret his decision. If he could convince his wife to take him back, the couple would need to consult a *mohallel* before the remarriage would be possible.

The *mohallel*, then, would have to marry the ex-wife for at least twenty-four hours. After consummating the marriage, the *mohallel* is supposed to divorce the woman. She would then be free to marry her original husband for a second time.

This role is most often performed by members of the clergy, who take on a kind of middleman role. In a way, Khomeini was a *mohallel* for Iran. He was brought in as the people of Iran were divorcing themselves from their government. In the interim, he was to allow a new leadership to form and then remarry the populace to its new government. Finally, his task would be completed and he would step out of the picture.

Something happened, though, when he arrived in Tehran on February 1, 1979. He witnessed a crowd of three million Iranians surrounding the airport and shouting, *"Agha amad!"* (The respectable man has arrived!) and *"Allahu akbar"* (God is great). The *mohallel* decided to keep the wife.

The years immediately following the revolution were difficult for many Iranians, but especially for the women. Before Khomeini had taken power, he spoke of women as brave leaders of the revolution. He promised them freedom once he led the revolt. But, as soon as he became head of the Iranian government, he declared polygamy legal again and revoked women's freedom to dress.

Homa was appalled by the laws of *hijab,* the Islamic dress code for women, which were being resurrected and enforced. These new laws required women to cover all parts of their bodies, with the exception of the face and hands, in public. Initially, the laws were restricted to government properties and bureaus. Eventually, however, the laws were expanded nationwide.

What exactly the dress code was, was open to interpretation. To follow them strictly, a woman would have to wear dark socks, long pants, a dark turtleneck long-sleeved shirt, and a long dark cloak cov-

Homa (**right**) in third grade and Parvin Darabi in first grade.

Homa's Islamic wedding ceremony. Parvin Darabi is first from left.

Homa in 1968 following her graduation from medical school. (Abbas Hashemi, Tehran)

Top: Homa and Uncle Hossain.

Homa and her husband, Mohsen, in 1967.

Right: Crowd including Parvin Darabi (in front without head cover) cheering Homa following her speech at a rally at Tehran University in the fall of 1963. (Courtesy of the Dr. Homa Darabi Foundation)

Left: Women in Evin Prison. (Courtesy of the Dr. Homa Darabi Foundation)

Above: Homa in Tehran in 1991.

Homa in the summer of 1993 in Tehran with family. **Standing:** Romin Thomson, Parvin Darabi. **Seated, left to right:** Grandma Aziz, Homa, and Eshrat Darabi.

ering herself from head-to-toe. A loose interpretation of the laws would require a woman to wear dark socks, a long-sleeved shirt, a long skirt, a scarf to cover her hair, and a long coat to cover her body.

Of course, these laws are often the most talked about throughout the world. They are a quickly recognizable symbol of the treatment of women in Iran. Proponents of the rules often argue that they are designed to protect the dignity of women and to prevent the male population from some sort of "excessive fornication." Nevertheless, beneath the surface and beyond the laws of *hijab* existed nationally sanctioned rules of law which were much harder to absolve. For example, in court, the testimony of a man was equal in value to the testimony of two women. Islamic women could not serve as judges. A woman could not travel, work, or go to college without the permission of her husband. The unilateral right to divorce was reestablished, meaning a man could divorce one of his wives without even bothering to tell her. In family court, mothers are not granted custody of their children unless the father and grandfather refuse custody.

From the beginning, Homa protested the establishment of the Islamic Republic by participating in demonstrations with other women and speaking out. She demanded that democracy be instituted as it had been promised.

In 1980, Bani-Sadr became the president of Iran. Homa arranged to speak to him as a representative of an organization of women. She approached the president about the laws that were being implemented. She told him they were unfair and archaic.

Bani-Sadr was a dedicated supporter of Khomeini's laws. His response to Homa was simple. He told her the rules of *hijab* were good for women. They would protect women. They protected them because the hair that grew from a woman's head evoked powerful rays that effectively hypnotized the men around them. Covering the hair prevented surrounding males from being overcome by their animal instincts.

Throughout this time period, Homa continued working for the university and in her private practice. However, her involvement in politics was gaining momentum. For a while, she was convinced that she could make a difference. She believed she could succeed in having the most oppressive laws repealed.

However, her confidence was shaken after Iraq attacked Iran late in 1980. The focus of the Iranian public quickly shifted from promoting domestic freedom to winning the war and supporting the government. People quickly lost interest in much of what Homa was fighting for. Many considered her actions inappropriate in light of the fact that they did nothing to promote the war effort. Indeed, they were perceived as a distraction from the movement.

She gave up nearly all hope when the first prime minister under Khomeini made a public speech on national television. He said that he, himself, had looked into the moon and seen Khomeini's face. The public reaction was incredible. Many people followed those words as if they were divine. Millions of Iranians were uplifted by the thought that their leader's face was depicted on the moon itself.

When Homa witnessed the impact of the statement, she knew she was working against an immense force. She could not understand why public reaction was so strong. She decided to give up most of her political involvement and focus her energies on her profession.

Her protests would now be reduced to subtle comments at medical conferences and she would use her classroom to instruct the youth of Iran on whatever values of freedom she could while teaching her subjects.

Chapter 19

Our Ailing Father's Last Request

I saw Homa again in 1984. I had moved to northern California. Our mother once again was living near me. Homa was in the United States for a medical conference and stopped in to see us. She arrived in the afternoon and we spent time together catching up on all the things that had happened since we saw each other last in 1978.

"Do you know what Dariush did?" she asked me.

"What?" I knew Dariush as the head of the Pan-Iranist party. Homa had been a member of this group ever since she became involved in politics in the late fifties.

"Right after Iran declared itself an Islamic republic and reinstated polygamy, he took a second wife."

"You're kidding! You mean he married another woman without divorcing Parvaneh? I thought he supported equality. What did Parvaneh say?" I asked. Parvaneh was our father's second cousin, and a friend of Homa's.

"Nothing. What can she do? She has no rights anymore."

"But Homa, how can you support him?" I asked, disappointed.

"I don't. I dropped out of the party."

"Good."

"All my life I have worked for equality and freedom for women and what Dariush did devastated me. I feel betrayed."

"So what do you do now?"

"Right now, I've been concentrating heavily on my practice. The situation in Iran has been a major disappointment. Whatever rights we had under the shah seem to have been taken from us. Now, women are regarded as second-class citizens.

"We're worth half what a man is. I feel like all the activism of the past three decades has been wasted. The Iran of today makes a thirteenth-century Iran look modern. I guess, right now, I'm just burned out."

"I thought this revolution was started and supported by women. What happened?" I asked.

"I'm not sure. We wanted it to be a revolution against inequality and injustice brought by the Pahlavi regime. Women did show up protesting in the streets, but they were there for all the wrong reasons. Many of them were paid.

"But Iranian women, like myself, never supported the implementation of Islamic rule. We fought for progress, but were simply out-numbered."

"Homa, I had no idea. I'm pretty ignorant of what brought the revolution about. Sometimes I wonder how it all happened."

"You're not the only one. I don't understand what happened either. People started out demonstrating by screaming "Death to the shah" and almost overnight people started hailing the Islamic Republic and shouting *"Allah O' Akbar."* Sometimes, now, at night, I whisper to myself, death to me for ever saying death to the shah."

The conversation trailed off for a while and then turned to other subjects.

"Homa," I said, "we have to talk about Dad."

"He's very sick. His cancer only gets worse," she spoke solemnly. She was in a remorseful mood.

"Why don't you let him die? He's been suffering for so long. The other day he said if it wasn't for you, he'd have died years ago." Homa used her influence as a doctor in Iran to insure that our father received the best care available to prolong his life. At a certain point, though, it started to depress him.

"Parvin, I'm a doctor, I've taken an oath promising to do everything in my power to keep people living. He's also my father and I can't let him die." She fought back tears while she spoke.

"Homa, I called him last week and he didn't recognize me. I had to remind him that he had a daughter and a grandson in America. It took him a while, and when he realized who I was, do you know what he said? He said 'Parvin, your sister is coming to see you in America. Please tell her that I want to die. I can't take the pain anymore. Tell her not to try so hard to keep me alive. Tell her I have a right to die.' "

Homa looked away while I spoke. She pretended not to listen.

"I think he's right. You should let him go," I persisted.

After a while she looked toward me again. "I can't." Again, she turned her head away. "Only God can take a life. I cannot be God." She was getting frustrated.

"I know that. But God had nothing to do with the advancement of medical technology. It's to the point now, that we can keep people technically alive for years. You even used to say that life is not worth living if you can't comprehend your environment. The only thing Dad can comprehend is pain. He's suffering. If you just let him be he can die a natural death."

"Parvin, as a person I agree with what you're saying, but as a doctor I will not neglect my patient!" By this time we had both become very emotional. We found something else to talk about and the day went on.

About three weeks later, Homa had gone to Ohio. From there, she called me with horrible news.

"Parvin?" She sounded weak, as if she could barely mouth the words.

"Homa? What is it? Why are you so upset?"

"He died, Parvin." She started crying uncontrollably.

"When?! Oh my God, when did this happen?" I started crying also.

"While I was with you," she said.

"What?!" I couldn't believe it. "Why didn't someone tell me?! I've been trying to call him, but I couldn't get through. Somebody should have called, though! Why didn't Mohsen or Hossain?!" I spoke slowly and in broken sentences, because I was so distraught.

"Hossain wanted to tell you, but Mohsen decided against it. He didn't want to disturb my vacation in the United States."

"But, Homa, he was my father, too. Why would your husband make a decision like that on my behalf?"

"I don't know." Her voice was still weary, "Dad's been gone for almost twenty days now. The day I left Tehran he fell into a coma and he died three days later."

"He was dead when you and I were fighting over his life?"

"He was already gone."

"How did you find out?"

She talked in a whining tone, as if she was an injured child, crying, and trying to explain how she got hurt. "I kept calling Mohsen and asking him about Dad and he told me that he was in the hospital. I finally called Mohsen at the hospital and told him to let me talk to our father and then he told me."

"I'll never forgive your husband for not letting me know that our father was about to die. I might have been able to see him one last time had I known."

"But Parvin, you're a U.S. citizen and you can't come to Iran. Mohsen thought it would be too dangerous for you to come." She was defensive. Both of us started to forget our grief and started fighting with each other.

"Regardless, I should have been given the opportunity to make that decision. At least I could have said good-bye to him by phone."

"He was comatose. He couldn't have talked to you over the phone," Homa replied.

"That's according to Mohsen. We don't know the truth for sure. It wouldn't be the first time he's misled me."

"What are you talking about?!" she responded aggressively.

"Do you really want to know? In '77 when Dad came to Orange County to spend a month with Romin and me. He ended up leaving after three days because Mohsen called and said that your younger daughter was very sick.

"Did you think I didn't know about this? I called Dad the next day because I was worried about your daughter. He said nothing was wrong with her. Mohsen lied then and you covered for him. He's probably lying now. Only this time, he's doing it to both of us.

"To see Dad one last time or to attend his funeral was a decision I should have been allowed to make."

"Parvin, there's nothing we can do now."

I said good-bye in disgust and hung up the phone. I stood in my kitchen and felt betrayed. It seemed as if I had lost my family the day I left for America. I even lost Homa, in a way.

I kept thinking that if Homa had not called Iran and insisted on talking to our father, we still wouldn't know. It was the same treatment my family gave me when Grandma Madar passed away. I tried to find some logic to justify it. None seemed to exist. He was my father, too. I had a right to know that he was dying.

After hearing the news, Homa left for Tehran with our mother to take part in his fortieth-day memorial services. It is traditional in Iran for people to mourn the death of a loved one on the third, seventh, and fortieth days following the person's death. Subsequently, graveside services are held every year on the anniversary of the person's death. I stayed in California and tried to keep myself isolated from everyone else. I was still angry.

Chapter 20

A Stranger in Her Own Home

Homa spent the next three years teaching and working in Iran. In our conversations she spent much of her time complaining about the ongoing war with Iraq. Every day the war effort dominated the headlines. In addition, living in Tehran was dangerous. Bombing raids were carried out periodically and no one knew where the attacks would strike.

Those were tense times for Homa. I often wondered why she didn't leave the country and find a safer place to live. I wanted her to come to California, but she refused. She knew her patients at the clinic needed her, perhaps now more than ever.

She was also treating many of the soldiers who were returning from the front line with severe physical and psychological problems. She empathized with them dearly and refused to abandon them.

I can't underestimate the impact wartime had on Homa. She was upset by the fact that no one wanted to focus any attention on the domestic problems caused by the strict new religious guidelines. People's homes were being randomly searched to find any forbidden items (recordings of Western music, videotapes of movies, alcoholic beverages, books, magazines, perfumes, makeup) and possessions were

171

being seized regularly because they conflicted with what the government considered to be the Moslem way of life. Nobody seemed to care about these invasions of privacy. People were obsessed only with the war.

In addition, Homa found herself treating soldiers at the hospital who had returned from the front line wounded, only to watch them be sent back to battle. If they returned a second time, they were usually in body bags or crippled for life.

The despair which surrounded her had a major impact on her mental state. Throughout our conversations, I could see that she was becoming burned out. I wanted badly to help her.

In 1987, I asked Homa to meet me in Germany. At the time, I was providing electrical engineering consulting services to a corporation in that country. I wouldn't make a trip to Iran because of the war and because the government wouldn't recognize my dual citizenship. When I became an American citizen, I became an enemy.

Homa flew to Frankfurt to meet me. With a friend of mine, I picked her up at the airport. The three of us went to Munich to relax for a couple of days. We stopped at an outdoor restaurant in the Marienplatz and talked for a while.

I noticed, this time, that Homa was depressed. As we drove through the countryside, she didn't talk much. She didn't smile much, either.

At the restaurant, I pushed her. "Homa, What is it? You seem pensive. What's on your mind?"

She looked toward me and took a deep breath. "Parvin, I don't know what to do. I am not happy with my life right now." She sounded horribly distraught.

"What do you mean? What's wrong?"

"The problem is getting worse. I don't think Mohsen is interested in me anymore. He works constantly and refuses to take any time off. We're hardly ever intimate. It bothers me."

"What do you mean? Is it you or is it another woman? Is he having an affair?"

"I don't know. I don't think so, but he is not interested in sex at all. No matter what I do, he just lies still, like a corpse." I could tell she was humiliated by the conversation.

"You're too young to give up your love life. Can you see a doctor? Maybe he's got a problem."

"I don't know. Sometimes I get frustrated, and I have to leave the bed. I've spent a lot of nights in our living room on the couch."

"That's awful," I said.

"I get harassed by the family, too. Almost everyone knows the problem. Mom constantly urges me to change my behavior. She thinks I shouldn't leave the bedroom so often."

"I can't believe this. You're both forty-seven. Your children are grown. You and Mohsen are doctors and you should be enjoying yourselves. You've waited too long for this freedom."

Homa's negativity about her relationship with her husband spread to almost every other part of her life.

"My children don't care about me either," she said. "Mohsen has raised them like *havou*. He's always bought their love with money. If they ask for something and I say no, he gives them his blessing and the money to go ahead with what I was against."

Comparing her children to *havou* was a shocking statement. *Havou* are women married to the same man who compete against one another to please their husband in order to get a little more money or a better meal from him.

"Homa! Come on now, aren't you exaggerating? How can your daughters compete with their mother for the love of their father?"

But her depression spread like a mental wildfire. "I have no control over my own home. When I'm there, I feel like a stranger to my own family. There's nothing I can do about it. I'm like a caged bird. If it wasn't for work, I don't think I could survive."

"What about divorce? It's always an alternative. You're a beautiful woman, a doctor, and an American citizen. You could find another man easily. One that would appreciate you and understand your needs. There's no reason for you to be so miserable. Come with me back to the United States and start a new life."

"I can't do that. Even if I wanted to, I can't get a divorce with these laws. Anyway, my daughters are going to college now. A divorce might cause problems for them. Besides, I don't think I'd see them very often if I left Mohsen. I had the chance a long time ago and I didn't take it. It's too late."

"Homa, what happened back then, anyway? Why did you go back in '76? I always thought you were going to divorce Mohsen and stay in the United States with your children." I had been wondering for a long time.

"If Mother had left me alone, I might have managed my own life. But she came and pleaded with me to return.

"In Iran, she warned, Mohsen could easily find another woman half my age and start a new family with her. He'd have new children and forget about our daughters. I would have to spend the rest of my life alone and our children would never have a father. Mom said I shouldn't risk my daughters' future for my own selfishness."

"But those are mostly cultural stigmas. Why would any of that matter if you stayed in the United States?" I asked.

"Children need stability. They need two parents and divorce destroys the environment they need. Remember what our mother did. Had she divorced our father when we were young, I don't think you and I would be meeting each other in Munich today. The fact that we are who we are is because she sacrificed part of her life for our well-being."

"But Homa, things have changed since we were children. I agree that children need stability, but they also need a loving home where both parents act in concert and do not compete for the love of their children. Something must have gone terribly wrong if you feel like a stranger in your own home."

"Maybe I shouldn't have let our parents have so much control over my life. I guess I shouldn't have brought Mom to America with me to care for our firstborn. I just wanted to complete my education. I knew I couldn't continue if I stayed home. I've made so many mistakes that sometimes I wonder if I ever did anything right."

"Homa, what are you doing? You can't blame yourself for everything that hasn't worked out perfectly. Your only mistake was falling in love with the wrong man. He should have taken you away from the family so the two of you could be free, together."

"That was another problem. Whenever Mohsen and I agreed on

something, Mom or Dad disagreed. I've never been able to make decisions without conflict. Even if it's just a decision of what to eat for dinner."

"Homa, stop. Let's talk about something else."

She continued. "In the beginning, I needed our parents to help me while I completed my education. When I was through, their lives were so messed up I couldn't let go of them. Their lives were intertwined with mine. Without me, they had nothing.

"Mother's been suffering from mental anguish since she got married. It only got worse while we were in Maryland. I tried to help her, but nothing could be done. She was damaged as a child, when they forced her to marry our father at age thirteen. She never recovered. Now she runs around like a homeless bag lady, and there's nothing I can do for her."

Homa wouldn't stop talking. She flew from one topic to another.

"Father developed prostate cancer and he suffered more and more as time went by. I tried my best to keep him comfortable during the last two years of his life. I fed him, bathed him, and tried to make sure he wasn't in too much pain.

"You were in America, Parvin, away from all the problems of our family, the war, and the revolution. I've lived through it all.

"You don't know what it's like to live every day under a constant bomb threat. You can't imagine how it feels to be a doctor without medicine for your patients. Every day I see young children returning from the front physically and mentally devastated from the war. You only read about it, but I see it. I live with it.

"And over all of this is the memory of the Islamic Revolution. It's left the country in the Dark Ages. All it's brought our people is poverty and misery. When I think that I was in favor of a revolution, it makes me sick. You have no idea what kind of atrocities are committed today. What they are doing now would make the shah look like an angel.

"Young girls who speak out against the government are raped before they are executed. The government believes that if a virgin dies, she goes to heaven, while nonvirgins are not allowed in. That is their justification for raping the girls before the execution.

"Women are stoned to death for adultery," Homa continued. "You should see what it looks like when they stone people. I'll tell you what happens, but you won't believe me. If they catch a married woman having an affair, the couple will have to be punished. Often, the punishment chosen will be stoning.

"Their bodies will be wrapped in bandages and their arms and legs will be tied so tightly that they won't be able to move. Then their bodies will be covered with sheets so that they almost look like mummies. They are taken outside where people are digging holes to put them in. I'm not talking about one or two soldiers or government agents. I mean there will be thirty, fifty, or a hundred people out there helping to dig the holes and to stone the victims." Homa wiped a tear from her cheek and continued talking.

"They stand the bodies up in the holes so that they are buried from the waist down. It seems strange, I know, but the bodies have to be buried like that so they don't fall over as they are being pelted with stones.

"There are rules for the stones, too. It can't just be any rock. The stone has to be big enough to really hurt the person, but not so big that it would kill them in one throw. Can you believe that? These people are sick." I started to feel ill.

"It gets worse, though. Once they start throwing the stones the excitement that builds is appalling. The people can't throw the rocks fast enough. They all stand in a circle about fifteen feet from the bodies and throw one rock after another as quickly as possible until the bodies have been hit so many times that the dirt in the hole loosens and the bodies slump over on their sides. Then the people gather around the bodies again. One group of people holds them while the other group fills in the holes. Then, the beating starts again.

"After a few rounds of this, the sheets and bandages start to tear and blood spills out onto the ground. When the people figure out that the couple has died, they bury them and walk away. Even that part is disgusting. There is no doctor present to make sure that the person is dead. Sometimes the victims are still alive when they are covered with dirt.

"As the people leave the stoning, they laugh and talk and tell stories like they are returning from a trip to the carnival."

I was in shock. I couldn't comprehend the kind of violence she was describing.

She continued. "Now, in Iran, men are hanged for having a drink. Women are given one hundred and fifty lashes of the whip for wearing makeup. They even killed Mrs. Parsa."

"What?! Faroukhlou Parsa?! The principal of our high school?"

"Yes. She was also the minister of education under the shah. She was the first female minister and they killed her."

"Why?!"

"They shaved her head and threw her naked into a gunnysack and then shot her. That's what people say."

"But why?! What did she do?" I was shocked. I loved the woman. She inspired me to study mathematics and I owe my career in engineering to her.

"They said she acted as a madam for the shah and other men in his cabinet. She arranged for them to have sex with young girls."

"Was there any proof? Did she have a trial?"

"Are you kidding?" she said. "Our tribunal judge, Sadeq Khalkhali, believes that protecting human rights entails liquidating unsuitable individuals so that others can live free. He says the revolutionary courts were born out of the anger of the Iranian people, and these people will not accept any principles other than Islamic principles.

"According to him, there is no room in their courts for defense attorneys because they only quote laws to pray for time, and this tires the patience of the people."

"So that's what happened to Mrs. Parsa?"

"Yes. Khalkhali decided she was one of the unsuitable people and so he had her executed for the good of society."

"Oh, let's stop. I'm feeling sick."

We stopped talking for a while and just sat there and stared at the people passing by. I cried quietly as I thought of the loss of Mrs. Parsa. She was a woman that succeeded in a place where women weren't supposed to succeed. When I learned about her becoming the first female cabinet member, I felt like I could do anything with my life.

I wondered what killing her might have done to the hopes of the young girls in Iran.

After a few minutes, Homa started talking again. Finally she spoke of more uplifting topics. She told a few of the popular jokes about the Islamic Republic and its leaders, and I gave her a sampling of my best ones. Still, the dismal mood remained.

We spent the next few days at a friend's home, and then I had to return to California. Before I left, Homa brought up some issues regarding our inheritance.

"I want to sell the house and the land we inherited from our father. Mohsen and I need the money to invest in our medical clinic."

"But I can't sell them right now," I said.

"Well, we have to; we need the money. With Uncle Hossain's help, we've gotten everything approved by the government. All we need is for you to come to Tehran to sign the documents. We both have to be there for the sale to be final."

"Are you crazy, Homa? I'm not going to Iran. It's too dangerous. I might have risked it to see my father, but do you really think I'll come there to sell some property?"

"Well, I don't know what else to do," she said.

"Well, don't sell the properties. Have Hossain send me an appraisal of the house and the land and I'll pay you half their appraised value."

"If they find out you're an American citizen they'll confiscate the properties. You understand that, don't you?"

"I know, but I'll take the risk. I think the situation will change and I'll be able to go back one day. Besides, the properties will appreciate in the future and so I want to keep them."

That was the end of our time together in Germany. Homa returned to Iran and continued working as she had. Conditions in the country were improving slightly because the war appeared to be coming to an end.

Chapter 21

Family Hostilities

In 1988, Homa came to the United States for a convention in San Francisco on child and adolescent psychiatry. She arranged to stay for a while so we could spend some time together. We had just returned from the airport when she started talking about our inheritance.

"Parvin, we finally managed to sell the house, but we had a hard time with you not being there," she said.

"But Homa! Why did you sell it! I told you I'd cover your half." I was surprised that she went ahead and sold the house. But I can't say I didn't see it coming.

"But the government would have taken it from you," she replied.

"But that was my risk."

"Hey! It took a lot of effort to sell this house with you not being there. Now, instead of thanking me, you're mad at me."

"Why should I thank you? You sold a house that I asked you not to sell. I even offered you your share of the money. Sometimes I feel like you think I don't even exist."

"Mohsen didn't think you could come up with the money, so we decided to sell the house."

"What does he know?! How does he know whether I can afford it or not?"

"We just figured, as an engineer, you wouldn't have the money."

"This was our inheritance. You could have asked me about the money. You could've at least given me the benefit of the doubt."

"Well, it's sold now and there is nothing we can do about it. I have a list of expenses for the house and for our father's funeral and these amounts will be subtracted from the proceeds."

"Where's the money then?"

"Your share is safe in my account in Tehran. I can give it to you whenever you want it."

"Well, I want it now."

"The money is in Iran. When I return, I can send it to you. You just have to trust me."

"Why? When you couldn't trust me enough to pay you for your half of the house? How can you expect me to trust you now? You're starting to sound like our mother, Homa. She always says money should not be a concern between mother and daughter. She claims there shouldn't be a difference in the dollar given to her by me and the one given to me by her. Of course, she only applies the adage to *my* money." I wanted to trust her, but I couldn't figure out how they managed to sell the house without me.

The next night when I came home from work, Homa and my mother were sitting in the living room talking with two guests—a friend of our mother and her son. The visitors surprised me.

The three ladies were discussing the possibility of matching Homa's eldest daughter, Azita, with the son. Azita had come to the United States in 1985 to study at Ohio State University. The discussion made me ill. I couldn't understand why an educated woman like Homa would want to arrange a marriage for her daughter.

I always thought times had changed since the days when arranged marriages were the custom and yet, here, in my living room, was evidence that some things never change.

The visitors left after a dinner that I hastily prepared and Homa and I were alone with our mother.

"Why would you guys do this?" I asked. "Why can't you let Azita find her own husband?"

Immediately, Mother jumped to the defensive and started screaming. Homa and I knew to ignore this and keep the discussion between us.

"Her father wants her to get married," Homa said. "We don't want her to be alone in America. It's no big deal if they happen to like each other. Mohsen's all for it."

"Is Azita for it?"

"We don't know. We haven't discussed it with her yet."

"A girl has to get married," our mother interrupted.

"Why?" I asked. "Some women never get married. But if she wants to, she'll meet someone at school or at work and can decide for herself. Why are you trying so hard to give her away?"

"I'm not trying to give her away. It's just that the sooner people get married the better off they are. They expect less of each other. I don't know, sometimes I think an arranged marriage can be better. Maybe parents know what's good for their children."

"God! I can't believe this is you talking. You're making me sick."

"Then I'll leave you alone so you won't be sick anymore."

Homa grabbed Mother, who was still hysterical, and left for her apartment. A few days later, Homa returned to Iran and we continued communicating by phone during the next several months.

In the fall, I spent two weeks in Germany. I was just returning from the trip when I received a call from Homa. She was in Ohio with Mohsen. The two of them were on a sabbatical from their positions in Iran and they were working near Columbus.

"I called to let you know that Mohsen's sister-in-law, Angela, has invited you and Romin to Columbus for Thanksgiving once again. She called while you were gone, but obviously you couldn't respond. Anyway, I think you better call and let her know your plans."

"All right, I will."

The next day I called Angela from work. I thanked her for the invitation and told her I had to decline because I wouldn't be able to get a flight on time.

"But Parvin," she said, "Please try to get a flight. We had so much fun with you last year. I've arranged for you and Romin to stay with us. Romin can stay with our oldest son and you and I can spend some time in the galleries downtown."

"Okay, I'll see what I can do. But if I get a flight, I'll get a hotel room for Romin and me so you don't have to disturb your son."

"No, please, I insist. We'll pick you up at the airport and you can both stay with us."

I did get a flight and I called Angela back to accept her invitation.

Romin and I started arranging things for our trip. I guess I was naive to think that everything would go smoothly. My sister called.

"Hello?"

"Parvin, why did you accept Angela's invitation?" Homa was angry. "Mohsen is devastated. He wants to know why you're staying at his brother's house?"

I didn't know what to say. "Well, they invited me."

"Mohsen says they invited you for Thanksgiving dinner and now you've planned to spend the weekend with them. He's very angry. He won't stop yelling. He wonders why you would stay at his brother's when he doesn't. Please, Parvin, do something. He's yelling at me. Please cancel your trip."

"But, Homa, why didn't you tell me this when you called? You could have asked me not to accept in the first place."

"Mohsen was sure you wouldn't find a flight on such short notice. I don't understand it, but now he's angry."

"But it's not his decision. Angela invited me."

"Look, I just want to keep the peace. I'm sorry for all this, but I can't always rationalize the things my husband does."

I hung up because I didn't want to deal with my sister anymore. It was a frustrating conversation. I felt she didn't have a problem with me going there until Mohsen did. She wouldn't stand up to him.

I decided to return the tickets and was planning to call the travel agent when the phone rang again. It was my mother.

"Homa told me you accepted Angela's invitation for Thanksgiving. Why would you do that? Mohsen is very upset." I was hearing a broken record.

"So, what? She invited me and I accepted."

"You have to understand, Parvin, Mohsen is right. It doesn't make sense for you to go to his brother's house when your nieces are there."

"Well, you'll be happy to know that I'm not going. I know if I do, Mohsen will find some way to get under my skin and we'll end up ruining the holiday."

"Are you going to let them know?" she asked.

"Yes, I will call them."

"When are you going to call them?"

"I don't know. I have to think for a while."

"What are you going to say?"

"Mom, enough!"

I really didn't know what to say to Angela. I respected their family so much, and I felt ridiculous having to call them this way, especially when they had been so nice to me. So, on Thanksgiving Day I called and told them that the traffic was heavy and caused us to miss our flight.

I never understood why Mohsen was so uncomfortable around me. I've always been courteous to him and his family.

Chapter 22

Fading Glory of Bygone Days

In 1989, Homa had a change of heart. The war in Iran had finally ended and both of her daughters were living permanently in the United States. She and Mohsen still were not getting along, so Homa decided to try to make a living in California.

She found a job at the Veterans Hospital in the San Fernando Valley. She moved in with a cousin. The two of them had an apartment and Homa had purchased a car. To me, it really looked like she might stay for good.

Mohsen, however, was not pleased with his wife. He came out to California after Homa had been living on her own for nearly ten months. He wanted to take her back to Iran.

When he came, I flew to Los Angeles and invited Mohsen and Homa to an Iranian nightclub in Los Angeles, the Cabaret Tehran. There we had dinner together and watched a show.

Afterward, however, Mohsen was unappreciative. He seemed bored all night. It was as if he didn't want to be there. I felt I should have apologized for making them suffer through such an ordeal.

When we went home that night, I couldn't sleep. I was praying for my sister. I wanted her to have the strength to resist her husband's plea and stay in California. Here, she was independent, and she did not have to worry about being suppressed by any government or any man.

I thought it might be her last chance to leave her husband and make a life of her own.

Unfortunately, Mohsen was too convincing. Whatever he said to her, she believed him and she ended up returning to Iran before the summer of 1990.

I went to Iran with my son, Romin, for eighteen days in August 1990. By then, Iran had reversed its policy on dual citizenship and ended the war. I was free to return. It was an exciting trip for me because I wanted to see the family I'd left so long ago. I stayed with Homa and Mohsen in their home. They lived in one of the first high-rises built in Tehran prior to the revolution.

The building was known as the ASP building. It had seventeen floors, but their apartment was on the basement level. The apartment had three large bedrooms, three large bathrooms, a dining room, living room, and an unusually small kitchen. One side of the apartment was actually two stories below ground level because the structure rested on a hill. Thus, there were windows on one side of the house only. In the living room, a sliding glass door led to a patio. But a high cement wall surrounded the patio and blocked light from entering the main room. Therefore, the place was almost always cold and dark. This also made it impossible to ventilate the apartment. There was no air-conditioning either. The air was always thick, and it wasn't uncommon to find huge cockroaches thriving in the humidity.

The first time I visited their home, I was shocked to see that two such accomplished doctors would be living in such conditions. I also worried about my sister. I wondered what living in such an environment could do to her over an extended period of time. She needed more air and sunlight than the *dakhmeh* (a cold, dark, and small place—the name Homa had given to their home) could provide.

While we were in Iran, Uncle Hossain took us to the Caspian Sea in the north of Iran. I was excited about the trip because when I was young we used to travel north for vacations. I was anxious to see the area again. There were four of us on the trip—Romin; Hossain; his wife, Giti; and I.

On the way, I wanted to find a restroom, but there weren't any clean ones around. All the toilets were essentially mud-holes in the earth with or without cesspools beneath them.

I remembered this very well from my youth. Because there was no sewer system, it was the only way. Hossain told me I should wait until we reached the old Hyatt Hotel, which was on our way, and I could ask to use a bathroom in one of the guest rooms there.

He explained, "After the revolution, they tore out all the European-style toilets in the hotel lobbies, restaurants, airports, and public places and replaced them with Iranian ones. But most rooms in the old European-style hotels still have their old toilets."

"What does religion have to do with the style of toilet people should use?" I asked him.

"This is how it is now," he replied. "Now it's these people's turn to run the country. We have no choice but to accept it. They have the guns and the power and if we choose to object, they'll come after us in no time."

We arrived at the hotel and Hossain started scrambling around to find a room in the hotel for me to use. I was in the lobby looking around what used to be a magnificent hotel, when a woman dressed from head to toe in black came toward me. She grabbed my scarf and tried to pull it forward over my hair.

I pushed her back and asked her in English what she was doing.

"I was trying to correct your *hijab*," she answered in Farsi.

I told her to leave me alone because I was American, but she wouldn't stop harassing me. Hossain noticed this, and he came back to me. We had to leave.

I had to wait one more hour until we arrived at a hotel in Ramsar. I had been to Ramsar in the summer of 1957. It was the year when Homa fell in love for the first time. When I closed my eyes, I remembered the elegance of the ladies who walked on the beach in their colorful bathing suits and evening gowns. I remembered how the sound of laughter filled the air back then. Then, to use the hotel you needed to make a reservation months in advance. People from all over the world came to dine on the best champagne and caviar money could buy. They danced and gambled the nights away.

But now, the place was dead. The hotel was empty. We were one of two families that had made reservations. We checked in and I finally found a restroom I could use.

Still, this hotel was one of the finest in Iran. Nothing in it came from postrevolution times. There were old furniture and torn sheets. The paint on the walls looked old and faded. I was grateful, though, for the European bathroom.

That evening, over dinner, I asked my uncle, "Why don't we go to the beach like old times?"

"We can't. We can go to the beach, but you and Giti have to stay on a female beach while Romin and I go to the male beach which is on the other side of town."

"What about the pool? Can we go swimming together?" I asked.

"No. Not together. They have two pools. The female pool is covered, but the other one isn't. If you like, you and Giti can go together and I'll take Romin to the other one."

"But Uncle Hossain, we're related. Why do we have to be separated?" I answered.

"Honey, it's not my rule," he said. I could tell he was frustrated by all my questions. He probably wondered all these things ten years ago, and by this time, he was tired of the questions.

The hotel manager came over to our table for a while and we spoke with him. He was a tall man, well dressed, but with a desperate expression frozen on his face.

He complained about the lack of customers. He couldn't understand what caused such a major setback in his life. He described better days when the phone at the reception desk wouldn't stop ringing and he had hundreds of employees. Now, he managed the reception desk and the restaurant, and the maids were only part-time workers. The hotel was there but there were no guests to occupy the rooms.

It was nothing like I remembered. We left for Tehran the next day. It was too depressing to see such a dead city.

Before Romin and I left Iran, I threw a big party at the outdoor grounds of Evin Hotel in Tehran. I invited all of our close relatives.

About a hundred people came. The hotel was one of the oldest and most luxurious in Iran.

It had an Olympic-size pool surrounded by a large asphalt patio. Four to five hundred guests can be entertained easily around this pool. Before the revolution, the place was alive with music and dancing almost every night.

This night, however, there was only the sound of a clerk's voice advising women of the rules of *hijab*. Three other parties were being held at poolside that night. One was a wedding, where the male guests were standing outside by the pool and the female guests were inside one of the large conference rooms on the ground level.

It felt like the only laughter came from our guests. Homa was the life of the party, as usual, and she told jokes and entertained people throughout the night.

All the female guests had to wear long coats and scarves. I'll never forget the words of our cabdriver as Homa and I came to the party.

He said, "The *hijab* is just an excuse. Iran sold oil to China for barter trade and they had to buy fabric in return. The government didn't know what to do with all that fabric so they forced the female population to cover themselves with fifty yards of fabric marketed by the Islamic Republic."

Homa and I laughed at this for a while. It was the perfect beginning to a wonderful night. I had more fun with my sister that night than I'd had with her in years. She was vibrant and energetic and it reminded me of our youth together.

It was the last time I ever saw Homa happy. Romin and I left for the United States the next day.

Chapter 23

The Unwelcome Invitation

I kept in contact with Homa for the next several months. It was a very bad time for her, but I never realized it. In December 1990, she was removed from her position as a professor at the university because she refused to fully comply with the Islamic dress code. This was the most disheartening moment of my sister's life.

She never mentioned it to me. She was too embarrassed to tell me what had happened. I always told her that if she stayed in Iran, sooner or later, some religious member of the government would come after her. She always told me it would never happen. She was convinced that her colleagues in the medical field were above all that. I guess that when it actually happened, she couldn't talk to me about it because she thought I'd throw it back in her face.

Anyway, we continued talking about once every month and I could tell through our conversations that she wasn't the same. She was hurting, but I had no idea why.

In September 1991, her daughter Azita decided to get married. By then I had moved to Maryland to work on a project with my fiancé, Reiner Meier. My son was in college in California, so the two of us lived alone. It was a new chapter in both of our lives. It was the first

191

time we could be together in the United States. It was also the year I turned fifty.

Reiner and I were planning a four-day trip to the Caribbean to celebrate my birthday and to start our new life together.

I got a call from Homa, who was in Tehran. She wanted me to attend a wedding that same weekend. "Parvin! My daughter's getting married!"

"Really?! Congratulations! That's great! Which one?"

"My eldest," she said, proudly.

"Who's the lucky man?" I asked.

"I don't know him yet. He's a professor at the University of Montreal and he has a Ph.D. in electronics."

"Wow! Well, that's great. It really is. How did they meet?"

"Azita went to Montreal for a vacation. She met him there and they fell in love."

"Oh, that's great. Azita is such a precious young girl. I'm glad she found someone she can be happy with. Are you looking forward to being a mother-in-law?" I asked.

"Yes, I can't wait. I'm looking forward to meeting the young man. I want you and Reiner to be there also. Make plans to come to Columbus on the fifteenth of September."

I was happy for her, but I didn't think I could accept the invitation. I didn't feel like I'd be welcome at her daughter's wedding.

I had a wonderful relationship with my nieces, Azita and Soraya, for most of their lives, but very recently some specific incidents had torn us apart. While in Iran, Soraya and I had a disagreement regarding politics. She was arguing with my son about censorship, of all things, and I joined in to try and keep the argument from becoming too heated.

The result was that Soraya and I got into an argument. When she got frustrated, she became insulting. What she told me really hurt my feelings. She said the only reason people wanted to spend time with me while I was in Iran was because of my money.

Anyway, after the argument, I didn't speak with her again. I could see that she had built up a lot of animosity toward me.

The second incident involved her sister. Some time after my return to the United States, I was on the East Coast for a business trip. I had a weekend free, and so I asked Azita if she'd like to spend some time together.

She said yes and so I bought plane tickets for a Baltimore-to-Columbus flight. When I called Azita again, she told me she had talked to her father and learned about the argument I had with Soraya. She said it wouldn't be good for me to come because she had to stand by her sister.

I had the tickets already, so I called Angela, Mohsen's sister-in-law, and asked if she wanted to have lunch together one day that weekend. Angela insisted that I spend the weekend with her and her family, which, of course, I did.

Well, Azita didn't approve. She came to Angela's house and demanded an explanation for my behavior. She embarrassed me in front of people I care for dearly, and she managed to make the rest of my stay in Ohio miserable.

That was the last time I spoke to Azita. Now I was being invited to her wedding. I didn't know what to say.

"I'm sorry, I don't think I can come, Homa. Your daughters have made it pretty clear that they don't want me around. I think seeing them will bring back unpleasant memories. September 16 is my fiftieth birthday and Reiner and I have plans."

"But, Parvin," she insisted "you're her only aunt and you should be present when she marries."

"I know. I should be. But it's hard, because I don't think I'll be welcomed by your daughters and their father. You and I should just be sisters. We should forget about the rest of our families."

"Parvin, please come. Do it for me. I already have enough trouble with my husband and his family because of you. Please don't make it worse." She sounded tired.

"What are you talking about?"

"Well, they don't approve of your divorces. Mohsen says, 'Every time I see Parvin she's with a different man.' If you don't show up for the wedding, I'll never hear the end of it."

I couldn't believe what I was hearing from my own sister. She sounded so passive in the way she put up with her husband's judgments.

"Homa! It's none of your husband's business how many times I decide to marry. Anyway, if I shame you so much, then why should I attend the wedding? Imagine what they'll say when they find out I'm living with Reiner out of wedlock."

"They don't know. Mohsen and his family think you and Reiner are married."

"But we're not! Jesus, Homa, this is my personal life. It's nobody else's business."

"I know that, but Mohsen and his family are much more religious than ours. Divorce is unthinkable to them. It's a sign of weakness."

"A religion that claims it's wrong for a woman to divorce and yet a man can have as many wives as he wants. It's ridiculous!" I replied in anger.

"Parvin. You don't understand. This is their time in Iran. There's nothing anyone can do. The religious fanatics are gaining in strength every day." In her voice was disappointment, but the frustration that used to accompany these topics was gone. I wondered where Homa, the activist, had gone.

"Regardless," she said, "I want you to be at the wedding. My daughters are young and they make mistakes sometimes. Please come. I can't take anymore arguing."

"I'll see what I can do," I responded, and we got off the phone.

After the conversation, I decided that I had no intention of attending the wedding.

However, I started getting calls from almost everyone in my family asking me about my decision. Everyone expected me to go and they were afraid I'd blemish the family's reputation if I didn't. My mother said I should forgive and forget the altercations with Homa's daughters.

"They're children," she said. "They make mistakes. It's up to you to forgive and forget because you're older."

A gut feeling was telling me to stay away from the wedding, but I gave in after Azita called to apologize for what happened a year earlier.

I did end up living to regret my decision. I didn't get to see my sister that much because she was constantly having to attend to other guests. Homa didn't seem herself. She looked awkward, as if she wasn't happy to see her daughter get married. She acted as if she was pretending to have fun at the wedding. She walked around with a forced smile and when people spoke of the marriage, she struggled to find positive things to say about it.

She made it seem as though her new son-in-law was a disappointment. I couldn't understand that because he seemed like a nice gentleman. I didn't know what was wrong with my sister. She had waited years for this night to come and once it finally did, she was disappointed.

The day after the wedding, Reiner and I went to Mohsen's sister Sakineh's home to say good-bye before going back to Maryland. In the living room, we found Azita sifting through her gifts and grumbling because she couldn't figure out how to transport all those things to Montreal.

Homa was there, too, but barely talked at all. She sat on the couch with her arms folded and her finger-tips gliding across her lips. Her face was pale. She stared at her daughter, trying to bite her nails. Our mother was on the other side of the room complaining about her own problems and wondering why Homa wasn't speaking to her.

Reiner and I just looked at each other, bewildered, because we didn't know why everyone was so distraught. A woman had just been married the night before and all she could do was count her gifts while her mother sat alone. Homa looked completely isolated in thought. It was as if she could not share what she was thinking with anyone.

I finally left with Reiner because the scene was too depressing. When we finally got home that evening, we were both disappointed in ourselves for wasting time and money on such an excursion. Still, both of us were concerned about Homa. We didn't understand why she had been so depressed the whole weekend.

Chapter 24

The Black Shadow of the Chador

During the next months, Homa's mood slowly worsened. I started getting reports from people in Iran who said that she was acting strangely. Several people said she was complaining because she didn't like the man her daughter had married. It didn't make sense to me because Azita's husband was a charming, successful man. There was really no reason for her to dislike him.

At about the same time, I found out that Homa had begun the early stages of menopause. Mother worried about Homa because she believed it would be tough on her emotionally. Mother blamed everything that happened to Homa on her menopausal state. For that reason, she returned to Iran in February 1992 to look after Homa.

I learned from our mother that my sister was continuing to complain about her life. But no one ever told me that she had been fired by the university. The entire family stayed tight-lipped about that.

In June 1992, I returned to Iran on a business trip. When I arrived, my uncle brought me to his home for the night. Homa came over early the next morning to see me, but her mind was occupied. All she could talk about was her new washing machine.

"Giti?" she asked Uncle Hossain's wife. "Is your washing machine made by AEG?" Homa walked down the hallway of my uncle's house toward Giti's machine.

"Yes. Why?" Hossain's wife responded.

I also wondered why she would ask such a question.

Homa was squatting in front of the machine, opening its door and staring inside. "We just bought an AEG machine and it doesn't drain completely," Homa said.

"Well, I don't know if it's the same. You have to find the model number. You should contact the retailer for that," Giti said.

I wondered what had come over my sister. I'd never seen her involved in domestic chores. I don't think she had ever used a washing machine in her life.

"Look, Homa," I said, "not all machines are the same. I'll come to your place later and see if there's anything wrong. Now, let's talk about something else for a while."

I tried to ask Homa about her daughters and our family, but she wasn't really listening. She gave me quick responses and said everyone was fine. I could tell she was still thinking about her washing machine. Her face had an intense expression. She sat, constantly rubbing her hands together. It was as if this minor problem with the machine was bothering her on a deep emotional level.

We sat silently for a while. When some of Hossain's friends came by, we greeted them and sat down together in the living room.

"Froog Khanoum?" Homa looked at one of the newcomers. "Do you have an AEG washing machine?" she asked.

"Yes, we do. Why do you ask?"

"Because we just bought an AEG machine and it doesn't drain properly," Homa answered.

My sister was beginning to concern me. She couldn't get her mind off her washing machine. My sister was not the type of person that let herself be consumed with the details of domestic life. If something was broken, she called a repairman to fix it. She wouldn't waste time worrying about such things. And yet, here she was, unable to carry on a normal conversation because she couldn't stop thinking about a washing machine that wouldn't drain.

"Why don't you call the company and ask them to send you a

repairman? They can fix it for you. The machine has a warranty, doesn't it?" Froog suggested.

"I have called the company and they did send the repairman, but he says there is nothing wrong with the machine. He says the machine's designed to operate that way."

"Why don't you exchange it for another one?" Giti interjected.

"Mohsen won't take it back," Homa said.

"You can take it back. Didn't you buy it?" Giti asked.

"No. Mohsen bought it."

I wanted to know what was wrong with Homa, but I couldn't ask the people present. I asked her if she wanted me to go home with her to check the machine. She agreed and we left with our uncle.

In the car I asked, "Homa, what's wrong? You're not yourself today."

"Nothing. Nothing's wrong. I'm just nervous because I'm preparing a paper I have to present at a conference. This thing with the washing machine is creating a big problem, too."

"Why aren't you working today?"

"I don't work for the university anymore. I just have my private practice every evening for a few hours."

"What?! Why not?! Did you quit?" I asked.

"No. I was just getting too tired. Working in the evening should be enough. Our children are grown. Azita is married, Soraya is going to Ohio State, and Mohsen works all the time. There's no reason for me to work so hard."

I didn't know she stopped working at the university. I also didn't know why she was so apathetic about no longer having the position. She used to love being a professor there. It made her feel as though she was finally using her education to benefit Iran by nurturing young students in the field. I couldn't understand why she spoke in such a sluggish manner about being unemployed. Her facial expressions were dull, and she put very little energy into her words. This wasn't the sister I knew.

"But, Homa, I never thought you worked because of money. You always worked to help people. And Iranians need your help now more than ever with the shortage of good doctors. Why won't you work at the university? It's the reason you left the United States, isn't it?" In a way, I was disappointed in her. I disagreed with my sister's decision to stay in Iran, but I respected her justification. I was proud to have a sister willing to sacrifice a major portion of her freedom for the good of humanity.

Homa looked toward me, as if to explain something. "But—"

"Parvin!" Hossain interrupted. "Look at what the new mayor of Tehran has done to this city. It looks beautiful, doesn't it? He's planted trees and flowers. He's made parks out of neglected lots, and he's created playgrounds for children. What did you think about the airport this time when you arrived?"

Hossain's interruption puzzled me. He knew I was waiting for an answer from Homa, but he cut her off anyway. I guessed that he stopped her on purpose, and so I answered his questions.

"I've heard about the new mayor. You're right, the airport was much cleaner this time. It's been only eighteen months, but I do notice an amazing difference," I answered.

While Hossain and I talked about all the changes, Homa sat quietly and looked outside the window. She seemed to be daydreaming.

"Hey," I tapped her shoulder. "What are you looking at?"

"I don't know, Parvin. I don't know where to begin. Maybe later we can find some time to talk. Azita and her husband are coming this week and I have a lot to do to get ready for them."

When we arrived at Homa's apartment, I took a look at her washing machine. I didn't find anything wrong with it except that it had a gentler spin cycle than normal and so water wouldn't squeeze completely out of the garments. I showed Homa how to use the machine, and then Hossain and I had to leave.

When we got in the car, Hossain asked me not to talk to Homa about her position at the university.

"Why not?" I asked.

"She was dishonorably discharged from her position as professor." Hossain was talking to me, but his eyes were on the road as he frantically tried to steer his way through traffic.

"What do you mean?!" The words rolled off my lips and my heart sank. "What does that mean?! How did that happen?! I can't believe it! What is she going to do?!"

"She was transferred to a new hospital last year. The head physician at the hospital is very religious. You know Homa doesn't like to wear the more traditional type of cover and she can't wear socks because of her skin allergies, right?"

"Of course!"

Hossain looked frustrated. "The head of the hospital told her she had to comply with the rules of *hijab* under the strictest interpretation. He said if she didn't, she would be discharged."

"Oh my God, what did she do?" I asked.

"She told him she would rather die than wear a chador."

"Are you serious?!"

"Yes. Then, she gave a presentation at a medical conference at which the minister of health was present. In part of her talk she complained, 'Propaganda in our neighborhood tells us that *hijab* gives a woman her dignity, but there can be nothing honorable about forcing a woman to hide under a black sheet.' She also added that a woman is unable to do anything without the chador while she can do everything under the chador, even carry weapons. They decided she didn't fit in well and so they gave her a dishonorable discharge."

"Hossain, why would they do that? This country needs people like Homa." I paused for a moment. "I'm very worried. A few years ago, Homa told me her job was what kept her going. What's she going to do now?"

"We're all worried about Homa," he said, "and I don't think Mohsen will let her go back to America again. It was a mistake for her to come back. Now she's trapped. I think it's worse now because she always wanted her children to live in Iran. But Azita's husband doesn't want to live here, and it looks like Soraya won't come back either. I know that hurts Homa."

Hossain dropped me off at my mother's home in Tehran. I ended up staying there for the rest of my trip.

The more I thought about my sister, the more concerned I became. Being fired must have been extremely traumatic for her. She lost everything she'd spent her life working toward. She could no longer teach medicine. I knew how much teaching meant to her. It was her chance to repay the nation for her education. She was dedicated to training doctors to carry Iran's future. She wanted that more than any-thing.

Then, to be fired for such a pathetic reason, because she wouldn't cover herself from head to toe. It was all the result of a revolution she had supported. A revolution she wanted to see. I felt very sad for her. I knew she'd been cheated.

The next day Homa came over in the morning. The two of us sat together in our mother's living room. Homa was solemn. She seemed very depressed. I couldn't tell specifically why, but I now know what was ultimately bothering her. She sat very still and her eyes hardly left the ground.

"Homa, what's wrong? Why don't you tell me? Maybe I can help."

"I don't think anyone can help me. My life is so messed up. I don't know what to do," she answered.

"But you have everything, Homa. You still have your profession, your husband, your home. You have money. Your daughters are accomplished people. One has a master's degree and has found an accomplished husband. The other one is still studying. In a year or two, you'll have a grandchild. How can you be so sad?" I asked.

"Parvin, I don't know where to start."

"Start anywhere."

"Mohsen and I have been living like roommates for years now. We've never been able to reestablish intimacy."

"You mean nothing's changed since we talked in Germany?"

"Nothing. He's like a brother."

"Why haven't you left him?"

"I can't. It's not legal."

"You could have gotten a divorce while you were in America. Why didn't you do it then?"

"What good would an American divorce be? I'd have to stay in America the rest of my life. I'd never be able to come back here. I love this country too much to do that. I'd rather live the life I have than be forced to live outside Iran for the rest of my life."

"But do you love your husband?" I asked.

"Of course! Why do you think I am so miserable? I love my husband and I love my country and neither one of them is treating me properly. But I just don't think I can break away."

"I understand." It was always difficult for Homa to make decisions, and this was a very difficult one. We sat together for a while and drank the tea our mother prepared.

Homa started talking again. "There is the problem of my daughter's marriage," she said, as she held a glass to her lips.

"What's the matter with Azita's marriage?" I asked.

"We had no choice in the matter. They were married before," she said. "The ceremony came after the fact."

I was surprised, but I tried not to let it show. "So? What difference does that make? They liked each other and they got married without your permission. This type of thing happens these days. Do you remember when you got married?"

"No, it wasn't the same. Azita met her husband while on vacation. Then, he came out to Ohio, so they could get to know each other better." She was crying. "When he got to Columbus, Mohsen's sister told them to get married and then try to get to know one another. Azita was about to fly to Tehran, so without letting her father and I know, her aunt married them off. When she came to Tehran, she was already married." Tears were pouring down her face.

"Homa, don't think about these things. You know how backward some of your in-laws are. They don't believe in dating. They are too afraid of their daughters losing their virginity before they are married. Anyway, what matters is the fact that your daughter is happy. I think she loves him." I was holding Homa in my arms, trying to comfort her.

"Don't you think I have the right to be upset, though? What would you do if your son came home with a woman and she was his wife?"

I'd kill him, I thought. "I don't know, I guess I'd be upset. But eventually I'd have to accept it. I'd just want him to be happy. I don't know what else I could do."

"I don't either, but I don't even know if my daughter married for love, or because she felt it was time to get married and he happened to propose. I am worried because she's so outgoing and her husband is so quiet. Through the whole wedding, we never heard a sound from him.

It may be the wrong match. I just don't want her to feel as lonely as I do after all these years. I'm afraid she may be isolated."

Homa was right. Azita had married a very quiet man. He had a brilliant mind, but he was quite pensive. "Homa, you shouldn't worry. Azita is a clever girl she knows what she's doing. Just give them your blessing and wish them the best."

"Parvin, you have such a relaxed outlook sometimes. I wish I had that. I think you got the better genes from our parents."

"Homa, stop."

"I just worry about their future."

"You're their mother. You're supposed to worry."

We were silent for a while, and Homa tried to stop crying. Her mind, though, seemed stuck in a kind of catch-22. She went from one depressing topic to another. Her cycle of thought provided no relief.

"And," she sniffled, "I lost my job. I was released because of my bad *hijabi*. It was getting so bad at work. Once, the government arranged a Koran-reading competition for all the nurses. When one of the nurses in the ward told me she couldn't stay with a patient because she had to practice for the contest, I blew up at her. I said they should have competitions that test bedside care and reliability and not how well they read the Koran."

"It's terrible. Their priorities are with the religion first, and then the patients," I said. "I can't believe it's the same government you and your husband worked so hard to bring to power. Remember how you tried to convince me to leave America and come back for Khomeini?"

"Don't rub it in."

"I didn't mean to. It's just sad, that's all."

"This isn't the government we wanted. We fought for freedom and democracy. We thought Khomeini would give the government to the National Front party and go off to Gom to preach. We were fools, I wanted change so badly that I forgot to be critical of how it came. Now, I pay the price every day.

"I mean it!" she said. "Every day! I can't even teach anymore. These officials took away my reason for living. They're trying to break me! What else do I have in my life besides my students?! Who can teach them like I can? No one here, you know that! All those kids, those young brilliant minds, have to be abandoned by their professor because of a stupid dress code!"

"Oh Homa, I feel terrible," I said. "What about your private practice? Don't you still have that to work for?"

"Maybe. I feel like that's all, though. I look around me and see so many helpless people. At work, I try to treat them. There are so many."

"I'm sorry, Homa, I'm not trying to blame you. It's not your fault. This revolution would have occurred without you. Forces created it that are beyond our control. But that's not important. We have to look to the future."

"Maybe," she said. But she did not change her mood. She was drowning.

A couple days later, Mother and I were invited with Homa to her brother-in-law Karim's villa just north of Tehran. The northern border of Tehran is covered by the Alborz Mountains. Up there you forget about the arid climate that affects most of the country.

Karim's villa is beautifully set in those mountains. It is completely surrounded by a vast cement wall. Adjacent to the wall, on one side, is the notorious Evin Prison. From the balcony of the house, you can see the jail and some say that the cries of political prisoners being tortured can sometimes be heard.

When I went there in 1990, I had a conversation with Homa about the prison after I noticed the high walls and the watchtower overlooking the house. I asked her what they were and she told me they were part of the prison.

"Why would anyone want to live next to a prison?" I asked.

"It's not to my taste either, but Karim got a good deal," she said.

"It's worse than living next to a cemetery. At least with a cemetery you know everyone's dead. I can't understand having a home next to a prison where people are tortured for their beliefs."

"I don't like to come here," she said. "It makes me think of all the people who were executed for political and religious reasons before and after the revolution." Homa continued, "When executions take place, you can hear the shooting from here."

"Oh, God! That's terrible."

"Karim only uses the place on Fridays, though, and they don't execute people on Fridays."

When we got to Karim's, the sight of the watchtower brought a chill to my skin as I thought about Mrs. Parsa and how she was killed.

We went upstairs to the main quarters and our mother immediately joined the ladies in one of the front rooms. I greeted them briefly, and then went to the balcony where Homa was with most of the men.

I noticed immediately that Homa was being pressured by her father-in-law. He was angry at her for something she had done concerning the washing machine.

"A woman should have more respect for her husband," he said. "She shouldn't complain about him in public. Don't you think so?" He looked at me.

"Well, I wasn't here and I don't know what happened with the machine," I answered.

The old man leaned back in his chair and tasted his tea. "Forget about the machine. That's just an example. You consider yourself a knowledgeable person, don't you?"

"Sure." I was uncomfortable, because I couldn't see what he was getting at.

"Tell me. Do you think it's appropriate for a woman to complain about her husband to his family?"

"Sir, I told you I am not in a position to answer. I don't know what went on between my sister and her husband." I sensed something negative coming.

"Well, in general, what do you think?"

"In general, I don't believe that it's reasonable if people are disrespectful to each other in public."

Finally Homa interrupted. "Parvin, I don't like the machine. I want him to replace it with one that I can operate, and he refuses! We had an argument about it here this morning. Now everyone thinks it was my fault. But he brought the subject up!"

"Well, I really don't want to get involved in any family feuds." I said "It seems like this should be left between the two of them. I'm not a judge, so why don't we just change the subject?"

"Don't you feel your sister's behavior was inappropriate?"

"I told you, I wasn't here."

I was irritated. I got up and left the balcony to find the women sitting together inside. It was one of the first times I ever chose to be a part of a female conversation in Iran. They were talking about food, marriage, and children.

After a while, I asked our mother if we could leave, but she wanted to stay and continue talking with Mohsen's family. I never understood what pleasure she could possibly get from such company.

When we did leave, I asked Homa to come with us.

"Homa, why don't you come over for a while? I'd like to show you some of the things I brought from home."

"She can't. She has to go with Mohsen to his eldest brother's for dinner," said Mother.

"Why can't she cancel?" I asked.

"It's like a tradition for them."

"What do you mean?"

"I have to tell you later. We can't talk now."

We said good-bye to everyone and climbed into the taxi my mother had called earlier. Transportation is a major problem in Tehran. The city's population has tripled since the revolution, but the number of buses and taxis has stayed about the same.

To move around the city efficiently, you have to rely on agencies and have taxis pick you up. These cabs are called call-cabs and they charge a lot more than the taxis you hail on the street.

Many government workers purchased cars before the revolution and now use their cars as call-cabs in the evening to make enough money to feed their families. Our driver worked for the national telecommunication company.

Once we pulled away from the villa, I asked my mother why Homa had to be with Mohsen's eldest brother that night.

"You see, Mohsen's father always wants to be with his children on Fridays. Therefore, they usually gather for dinner on Fridays. But his oldest son and Karim haven't been on speaking terms for almost fifteen years.

"In order to keep everyone happy, the rest of the family meets at another brother's house for dinner on Friday evenings. This week it's Mohsen's eldest brother's turn. Next week it will be Mohsen's turn."

"You mean *every* Friday!"

"Yes. It's like a tradition, see?"

"What does Homa think about it?" I asked.

"There's not much Homa can do about it. It would be inappropriate for her to object to the wishes of his family. Parvin, this is the way it is here. When an elder wants you to do something, you do it."

"But it's so monotonous!"

"Sometimes they can get out of it. Sometimes there's an emergency with one of Mohsen's patients or some relative will be in town and they'll skip the meal. Still, almost every other weekend I work all day with Homa's maid, Khadijeh, to prepare dinner at Homa's for the group."

"Why do you have to do it?" I asked.

"Who else can? Homa couldn't do it, she's too busy. I've always done it for her. My mother helps, too."

"But it's a lot of work for you and Grandma. Why can't they cater dinner from a restaurant?"

"Mohsen doesn't like that. He knows it would be a lot more expensive."

"So, every Friday the family has to be together whether they like it or not?" I asked.

"That's the way it works here. A lot of families are that way."

"That's terrible. I mean, Homa should get some time alone with her husband on their day off."

We were out of the mountains now, driving through the city. The air was hot and muggy. We were sweating.

"Well, do they ever get away? Do they take vacations or go hiking or swimming or shopping together?" I asked.

"No. They never do those things." Mother thought for a minute. "You know, I don't think I've ever seen the two of them affectionate. I've never seen them kiss."

"That's sad. You know, Mom, I'm concerned about Homa. She's not herself."

"We're all worried about her," she said.

"I've never ever seen her pay so much attention to household chores. It's so weird to see her worked up over a washing machine. I don't think she's healthy. She's depressed."

"She's been quietly avoiding people ever since she lost her job. It was embarrassing to her, to be fired, I mean. I think she might also be struggling because she's going through menopause. It's probably temporary. We have to give her time."

"I'm not so sure," I said. "I want you to help her because I don't think her husband will."

"She says she's fine and she still works every evening."

"Well, I'm just worried," I said.

The next week my mother, grandmother, and I were invited to spend another Friday with Homa at Karim's villa. To get there, we agreed to meet at Homa's and drive with them.

We arrived at my sister's house at eleven in the morning. We were supposed to be at the villa by noon. It was a one-hour trip, so we were anxious to leave, but we couldn't because Mohsen was still working.

While waiting, I noticed a large box in the middle of the patio. I asked Homa about it and she said it contained two chandeliers.

"Did you buy them?" I asked.

"No. One of Mohsen's patient's just died and he left the chandeliers as payment for his bill. So this morning, before any of his heirs got them, the chandeliers were delivered here."

We sat down and waited for Mohsen. He didn't show up until about 12:20. Homa was furious when he came in the door. She asked him why he was so late.

He didn't answer. He came in the door, looked right past his wife, and surveyed the room with his eyes.

The first thing he said was, "Did they bring the chandeliers?"

"They're on the patio," answered Homa.

Mohsen rushed to find them and when he pulled them from the box called to Homa, "Bring me a screwdriver. I want to hang the chandeliers."

"But, Mohsen," she said, "your brother is waiting for us. We're already late. Hang the chandeliers tomorrow."

But he didn't listen. In fact, I'm not even sure he heard her. He stood on a chair in the living room and started pulling the old lamp from the ceiling.

Regardless of what Homa said, Mohsen was determined to work until he got the chandeliers installed.

I was getting frustrated, so I asked my sister if we could go without him and have him follow us later.

"I hate always having to go to places alone," she said. She looked at her occupied husband and then said, "Let's go."

On our way out the door, we heard the sound of glass shattering. I turned around and saw that Mohsen in his hastiness had dropped a branch of the chandelier.

It was after four when he finally joined us at Karim's. By then, we'd all finished lunch, napped, and were getting ready to enjoy some tea and snacks.

That evening, I shared a cab with my grandmother back to my mother's house. As we climbed in the taxi, my grandmother started talking about Homa.

"I feel sorry for her," she said. "Did you see what he did this morning? He got so excited about his chandeliers that he completely forgot about his wife and her family."

"I know," I said. "It was awful."

"He only likes to socialize with the men in his family. He refuses to have anything to do with us. Homa used to put on *doreh* parties." The *doreh* were parties among a group of friends that rotated each month from one person's house to another. Aziz continued, "She had to stop because it was too hard to get Mohsen to show up."

"Why wouldn't he show up?" I asked.

"It was hard for him to escape work on the weekdays, but he also never really liked parties. They were always opposites in that respect."

"Couldn't she have the *doreh* on a Friday so he could come?"

"Fridays have always been reserved for Mohsen's family."

"It's crazy," I replied.

The next night was going to be my last in Iran, so I arranged another dinner party at the hotel in Tehran. I had already packed, and it was up to my uncle to take me to the airport that night after the party.

Mohsen came late that night also.

Just as he had done two years earlier, the clerk was using his microphone to remind women of the rules of *hijab*. His voice was a constant interruption of our evening.

At one point, I was so fed up with the speaker that I stormed off to find his table. My mother started chasing me because she was afraid I'd end up hurting the man.

When I found him, I told him, "If I hear that Islamic reminder one more time, nobody here tonight will be getting a tip from my party. None of you! Not the waiters, the cook, the doorman, or the manager."

It was a persuasive threat. We never heard the clerk again that night. Later, I boarded my plane at Mehrabad Airport to leave for Frankfurt. As soon as the door of the plane closed, I took off my Islamic garb. It felt good to be free again.

Chapter 25

Behind the Walls of Depression

Five months later, Homa's disposition was getting worse. She was still very upset about losing her job. She missed being able to teach every week. She was having trouble staying away from her profession. I started thinking about treatment possibilities. If we could bring Homa to the United States, we might be able to treat whatever was ailing her mentally.

I called her daughter Azita to ask her opinion on the matter.

"Now, Aunt Parvin," she said, "don't get yourself involved."

"Azita, I am involved. Your grandmother called me two weeks ago and said my sister was in bad shape. She wants me to go there to see if I can help." I was upset with our conversation. I expected her to be more sympathetic.

"But my father says there is nothing wrong with her. He says she's making it all up. She won't get well simply because she doesn't want to."

"Azita, no one can fake a depression. She's not making anything up."

"You just don't know my mother. She can."

"Azita! That's a horrible thing to say. Your mother needs help. We should reach out to her."

"But Aunt Parvin, you just don't know what we went through last

213

summer when we were in Iran. She used to pace the room day and night. When she was too tired to pace, she would simply pass out regardless of where she was. Being around such a restless person was strange for me."

"That's why we need to help her. We need to break through her shell. She needs us. I think we should bring her here. Doctors in the United States have made incredible advances in the field of depression."

"Aunt Parvin, she's not suffering from depression! Regardless, there's no way she can come out here. I can't care for her because my husband and I live in a small apartment with very little room for her. My sister can't help either because she has too much studying to do. At the same time, you work, and I don't think you can dedicate your time to her.

"In Iran, however, she has my father to care for her, and the rest of the family is there to support her. It makes more sense for her to stay there."

"Azita, if Homa's problems stem from some kind of mental disorder, she won't need our help. She'll need to be admitted to a hospital that can provide her with assistance around the clock. We can arrange this here."

"But who would pay for it? Health care in America is too expensive. In Iran, she gets it all for free."

"Your mother has enough money to afford it. Besides, your father also has a lot of resources available. Plus, with Homa recovered, she can earn the money back in no time."

"Are you suggesting we waste the few thousand dollars my parents have saved?"

"How can you say that? Why would you suggest this money would be wasted if it is used to help your mother? What kind of talk is this?"

"I'm telling you, Aunt Parvin, my father says there's nothing wrong with my mother. Now, you disagree and your mother does, too. Who should we believe? The two of you, or a medical doctor?"

"I guess there's really nothing for us to talk about then."

Our mother called me several times to talk to me about Homa. She was trying to help her daughter, but nothing was working. Every week she would tell me frightening stories about my sister. She would detail the continuing decay of her emotional state. She would cry to me at times. She begged me to tell her what to do.

There were times when Homa would simply pace the hallway of their home with her hands fidgeting and grasping each other. She would murmur things under her breath constantly. "What am I going to do? Why did I mess up my life this way? What am I going to do?"

Mother's stories took their toll on me. I decided to take a trip to Tehran to see Homa. I wanted to evaluate her condition on my own. I never placed complete faith in any of my mother's opinions.

In the middle of November, on the day I arrived, Hossain, my mother, my grandmother, and I met at my Aunt Maryam's home to have lunch together. Homa was to join us. Shortly after our arrival, a call-cab dropped her off.

While we waited for her, Maryam took me aside in the kitchen to prepare me for my sister's arrival. "Look," she said. "I don't want you to be shocked when you see her. She's worse than she was when you saw her last, a lot worse.

"Please, don't give any horrified expressions when you see her. Just remember, her medication is causing most of her physical pain."

The warning, alone, caused me to break out in a cold sweat. Still, no amount of preparation could have been sufficient for what I was about to see.

Maryam's apartment was in the northern part of Tehran. She had a living room, dining room, and family room combined in one large L-shaped room on the main floor. My mother and I sat on the couch in the living room while Maryam and Aziz prepared lunch in the kitchen. We talked about a variety of subjects, but I was only concentrating on the anticipated arrival of my sister.

Homa walked through the front door. Maryam greeted her, and I almost didn't recognize her. She walked slowly! She'd put on a tremendous amount of weight, perhaps forty pounds. Her slender body now looked almost stubby. Once she sat down with us, she couldn't stop fidgeting. Her hands roved around her body making slight adjustments to her clothes almost constantly.

She was also trembling. Her body shook as she moved around.

Her lips also quivered, and for this reason, she spoke slowly to make sure she was understood.

Mother peeled an orange and placed it in front of Homa. Then she started peeling an apple. Homa quietly ate both while staring at me.

Her face was so blank that I wondered if she even tasted the fruit.

I never imagined that I'd ever have to see Homa in such a humiliating condition. I cried softly throughout our time together.

"Homa," I said, "I don't like seeing you like this. Why don't you come home with me this week? I can take care of you in America. I can take you to the Johns Hopkins Medical Center in Maryland and they can treat you. Or, if you like, we can treat you at Stanford Medical Center when Reiner and I move back to California. I'm sure either of those facilities can help you."

She waited before replying. I wondered if she was paying any attention to me. "Parvin, there's nothing mentally or physically wrong with me. Regardless of which doctor I see or which hospital I go to, I will not get well because I am not sick," she answered.

"Then what is it? Why do you act this way? What's changed?" I asked.

With her face now pointed toward the ground. "I've messed up my life and I have nothing positive to show for my time here. I'm not even a doctor anymore."

"What do you mean?" I asked. "If you want to be a doctor again, come to America. You can always practice there. Don't be so pessimistic. You've done a lot in your lifetime, and there's much more for you to do. Don't forget, you have two daughters and soon Azita is going to make you a grandmother. You know all this, Homa. Why do you act like—"

"Don't talk to me about my daughters. They don't give a damn about me. They only like me when they want something." She looked at me now, and she spoke in a slow, thick voice.

She sat still for a minute and then she spoke again. "This time Azita wants me to make curtains for her new apartment. But I have no idea how to do that." Her eyes were becoming glassy, but her expression remained fixed on me.

"What?" I asked.

"She wants curtains," Homa replied, and she folded her arms tightly around her waist.

"She wants you to make them here and ship them to Montreal for her? Don't they have those things in Canada?" I asked sarcastically, looking at my mother.

"She says they're more expensive there."

"Just give her the money and let her buy the curtains she wants. It would be easier on you."

But while I talked, a tear slid down Homa's face. She let it fall all the way to her chin and then drop onto her collar. She never wiped her eyes or her face. She acted as if it wasn't there.

"Parvin, you don't understand. Children like their mothers to do these types of things."

"You're not superhuman. Sometimes expectations are set too high. Just give them the money and remove yourself from the obligation."

"I don't think I should do that. Azita's already angry at me because I wouldn't put on a wedding reception for her last summer."

"You gave them one in Ohio, right?"

"Yes, and she wanted another reception in Tehran for all the friends and relatives who couldn't go to America."

"Why didn't her in-laws give them one?"

Another tear fell from her eyes.

"That's what I asked her. In my opinion, we gave the one in Ohio and it would be fair if they would have given the one in Tehran."

"Did Azita disagree?" I asked.

As she spoke, she released one of her arms and touched her hair. "She said his family couldn't afford it."

"What made her think you could?"

I was quickly distracted by Maryam who was calling me from the kitchen. She sounded as if she needed me right away, so I walked to the kitchen as fast as I could.

"What do you need, Aunt Maryam?" I asked her.

She had her hands in a large bowl as she was cutting up an eggplant. "Parvin," she said, "don't talk to Homa about Azita right now. It's a bad time."

"Why?"

She whispered to me with much force behind her words. "When Homa refused to have the second reception for Azita, a major argument broke out between the two. Azita ended up threatening to ask Mohsen to divorce Homa. The statement tore Homa apart. I think it confirmed her inner belief that the girls favored Mohsen as a parent."

How can a daughter say such a horrible thing to her mother? I thought. I remembered my conversation with Homa, when she compared her daughters to *havou,* as if they competed for their parents' love in exchange for money. It sounded ridiculous, but I couldn't explain Azita's behavior. It also explained why Azita wasn't sympathetic to her mother's dilemma when we talked before my trip.

While I was with Maryam, Mohsen had arrived and was sitting in the living room with Homa and our mother. He looked distracted, as usual.

I went to the living room and greeted him, trying to ignore my own feelings. We all sat together and talked while we drank tea. Mohsen took a sugar cube, dipped it into the tea, placed it in his mouth, and started drinking. I never liked sweet tea, and so I drank mine plain.

After a little while, I gathered the nerve to ask him about his wife. "Mohsen, I want to take Homa back with me. I want to try and help her in America. Will you allow her to come with me?"

He answered very quickly, without taking any time to think. "It's up to Homa. She's a free person." He turned to his wife and asked, "Homa? What do you think? Do you want to go to America?"

"I don't know," she said.

Mohsen responded to her in a loud voice that seemed almost apathetic. "Well, if you want to, you can. It's your decision. I won't stop you."

Maryam had finished setting the table for lunch, and she called to us, "Please come and have lunch."

As we rose to go to the table, Homa asked Mohsen about my proposition.

"Should I? What if I went?" She was slowly seating herself in one of the chairs around the table.

"That sounded like a yes to me," I said.

"Homa, it's your decision," he said.

"Now, Mohsen," I interrupted, "you know how hard it is for Homa to make decisions. It's not fair for you to force her like this. Just look at her. Look at her face. Look at her eyes. She's ashamed to be here! You shouldn't ask. Just get her a ticket and an exit visa and we'll leave next week."

At this, he exploded. He was standing at the head of the table, barking at me.

"Who the hell are you!?" he demanded. "You're not a doctor of medicine! You don't know what your sister needs! This is my wife. This is an Islamic republic. She has a husband, two daughters, and a son-in-law and as long as that's the case, *I'll* decide what she does and where she goes."

"Please! Mohsen, relax!" my grandmother interrupted him. "Parvin is just concerned about her sister."

He raised his voice. "I know what's best for my wife! I don't need any of you to get involved in our affairs! Is that too hard for you to understand?!"

Maryam pleaded with him. "Mohsen, you're tired. Please stay calm and have some lunch. We can talk about this later."

"No!" he persisted. "We have nothing to talk about. She needs my permission to leave and I won't give it. You'll just have to live with that."

"Look!" I screamed, "I know I'm not an M.D. but you're no psychiatrist either! You're a hematologist. I've been doing a lot of reading about depression, and I'm finding out that it has a lot to do with women going through menopause. I also know that America is a more advanced country. You can find medicine there that isn't available here. Anyway, if she comes back and her condition improves, she can practice again. No one's going to steal her right to practice because of any dress requirements!"

"You don't know anything. You only bullshit your way around your life. Your opinions aren't worth a damn! Homa is my wife. I know what to do with her.

"Homa, get up!" He started pulling Homa out of the chair by her arms. "Let's get the hell out of here." She hurriedly got up and took his hand.

The two of them started walking toward the door.

My grandmother called to them. "Please! Mohsen, sit down. We should eat."

"Parvin didn't want to say anything bad," my mother added. "She's only concerned. You shouldn't go right now."

Hossain also added, "Please, Mohsen, nobody meant any harm."

"I do the best I can to take care of my wife!" Mohsen said angrily.

"What do you mean?!" I demanded. "What have you done?"

Just then Mohsen stopped heading for the door and snapped back at me, "She's with her mother and everyone that loves her!"

"But her mother is sick, too. We all know that. She can't help Homa. Why can't you understand that?! Homa needs professional help!" I answered.

"Then I can hire her a nurse. She doesn't need any of you people. I'll take care of her myself and all of you bastards can leave us alone." He was looking at all of us.

"You don't have to start insulting us. No one here has insulted you!" I told him.

"I'll say what I want to. I want to get the hell out of this place." He continued toward the door, pulling Homa behind him.

For the next few seconds, I was the only one silent in the room. The sounds of my family begging Mohsen to calm down were overwhelming. But they only seemed to raise Mohsen's anger. He might have thought he had been ambushed. He might have felt we all invited him there to confront him about his wife. He was furious. Before he slammed the door and left, he released Homa and shouted at us, "I want all of you *Madar Ghahbeh ha* [strictly translated, it means "your mothers are whores"] to leave my wife and me alone."

At this, Uncle Hossain lost his cool and ran outside to attack Mohsen. The two of them stood nose-to-nose screaming at each other until Aziz and Mother separated them.

It was a tense moment; no one knew what was going to happen next. I'd never seen my uncle so angry.

Maryam held Homa aside. My aunt was weeping uncontrollably. Homa seemed unfazed. She'd been that way throughout the argument. She looked as if she was in a different world. I'd never seen my sister so passive in her life. If anything, she was apathetic to the conversation going on around her. It was astounding, because the conversation revolved around her future.

I stayed at the table and watched Maryam and Homa just inside the doorway. I could see Mohsen and Hossain outside. I felt as if I was witnessing a preview of what hell was going to be like when I died.

What was this tantrum about? I thought. I asked if I could take my sister to America. All he had to do was say no. Instead, he manipulated Homa's timid decision-making ability to his best advantage.

He was hoping she wouldn't be able to decide. When her response was ambiguous, he blew up. He must have felt like she might be ready to leave him once again.

When Mohsen took Homa and finally left, Maryam went with them. The rest of us sat down to lunch again. We were silent for a while, shocked by what had just occurred.

Mother got us talking again.

"Parvin, why couldn't you have waited till we ate to start talking about Homa?"

"Wait a minute," I said, "why am I to blame?"

"You know he's under a lot of pressure and having his wife like this isn't helping. You should be careful when you talk to him," she replied.

"When have we ever been able to talk to Mohsen without having him attack us. He always insists that he's right in his thinking. I'm tired of his attitude."

"We have to try and help Homa, though," Hossain added.

"I know. But we can't. She needs professional help. She can't get it here, from doctors who used to be her students. We have to get that through her husband's head. Actually, the best thing we can do for Homa is to let Mohsen assume all responsibility for her. If we stopped taking care of her all the time, he'd have to get her help. Or he could abandon the burden and leave her to me."

"No," my mother said. "I can't stop caring for Homa. She's my daughter. She needs help cooking and cleaning and, now, she needs my company during the day."

"Mom, what Homa needs is calm, quiet surroundings. She needs a place where she can find some peace. The company she needs has to come from people on her own intellectual level. You can't provide any of these things for her."

"I don't know. I can't stop helping her. I won't."

We started eating. After a while my mother started talking to me again.

"Sometimes, I don't know what to do. Mohsen never wants to hear anything I say. I have to fight just to get him to give Homa her medication on a regular basis."

Knowing my mother's belief that any ailment can be cured if you take enough pills, her statement about Homa worried me. "What medication?" I asked.

"He tries different things," she said. "Once, Mohsen had his sister ship an antidepressant drug, Prozac, to Iran for Homa. But it made Homa sick, so she had to be taken off the medicine."

"Mother, this is medication by trial-and-error method. It's wrong."

"There is nothing we can do. There's no law to protect her. He owns her," Mother said with a deep sigh.

"As it stands," she continued, "he has to give her permission to leave the country. You can see how he feels about that. If I could take her, I'd do it myself. But right now, all I can do is be there for her. I only hope that her condition is temporary. I want her to snap out of it one day. I keep waiting for that day. Every morning, when I see her, I look at her and wonder, Is today the day?

After lunch, we napped for a while. Maryam came back while we were sleeping.

When we awoke, I asked her about Homa. "How is she?"

"She was trembling. She didn't say anything. Once we got to their house, I fixed her some chicken kabob and put her to bed. I also made them tea, and then left because I knew they were to have dinner with Mohsen's older brother tonight," Maryam reported.

"Is that because it's Friday?" I asked. "Do they still live by that ritual?"

"Just be happy we got to see them this afternoon," she said.

"What about next Friday? Do they still host the dinner every other weekend?"

"Yes, and poor Homa starts panicking about it on Thursday morning. She paces the floors and wonders what to prepare. I don't think she sleeps well that night either."

"Can't Mohsen cancel these gatherings while his wife is feeling so bad?" I asked.

"He won't. We've tried to get him to cancel, but I think he feels it's best for Homa to be surrounded by people. He doesn't want to isolate her any more than she already is."

"But they can meet in a restaurant."

"She'd still be nervous, and Mohsen never enjoys eating out."

"Can't someone else fix the dinner and bring it over so Homa doesn't have to bother with it?"

"We tried that once. Eshrat called Mohsen's mother and asked her if she would make the rice while she prepared the dish to accompany it. But when Mohsen picked up his mother that evening, he became upset when she tried to bring the pot of rice. He asked her what it was, and she said it was rice. She told him she wanted Homa to relax for the evening."

"What happened?"

"He threw a fit and tossed the rice onto her front yard. Parvin, no one can talk to Mohsen about Homa."

"It doesn't make sense. She can't have peace in her own home," I said.

"I know. It's awful for her. I feel so bad. She even hates the house. She calls it the *dakhmeh*."

Chapter 26

A Rich, Poor Country

The next day Maryam and I had an appointment to see Homa's doctor. When we met with him, I introduced myself.

"I'm Dr. Darabi's only sister. I've come from America to see her and I'm thinking about taking her back with me. Her husband objects, however, and I wonder if you might be able to change his mind. As a physician, your opinion might mean a lot to him."

"If you are able and willing to take your sister to America, that could be a good solution. In America, they can give her the benefit of better medication and more facilities. Here, all we can do is pray for our patients because we have so little to give them."

He was a nice gentleman, with a pleasant disposition. He continued talking about Homa and what he thought was best for her.

"I will definitely talk to him. If he denies her this chance and something goes wrong with her, it will have been his fault. But I can't promise you I'll change his mind. He's a strong-minded person."

For the rest of my week in Iran, Homa visited me at our mother's house a few times during the afternoon. She would stay with us for a few hours, starting at about noon. On one Friday I spent there, she came early, and we spent the morning together.

She was lackadaisical. I wanted to talk to her to discover the reason why she was being distant. It wasn't easy for us to find time alone. Homa and I have never been able to discuss personal issues in front of our mother. She was far too judgmental, and her opinions were always based on her own life's experiences. Sadly, she could never be objective about any of our problems.

One day, I asked Homa to take a walk with me through the Park-e-Saii. We put on our Islamic robes and scarves, said good-bye to Mother and Aziz, and went walking.

Park-e-Saii is about three hundred meters down a hill, from Mother's front door. It is a lovely park with trees, flowers and walkways built throughout. It also has a small zoo with different types of birds and animals.

The two of us walked to the center of the park and sat on one of the benches. As we watched people walk by, I asked Homa about her husband.

"Homa, why don't you ask Mohsen for his consent to come to America?"

She leaned back against the bench and looked straight out across the park. "I don't know. I don't think it would help." She took a very long breath.

"I can't live in America." She raised her left hand and continued, "This is my country. This is where I was born. You know, our father, his father, and even his father's father are buried here. I guess I want to be here when I die, too." She looked around us. "Did you see the snow-covered peaks of the Alborz Mountains this morning? Things like that give me energy. I can't give them up."

"But Homa, why can't you live in America? I've been there for the past twenty-eight years and I've grown to love it. I miss it when I leave, for even a few days. You can be the same way. You can learn to love a second home, if you try."

"It's different," she insisted. "You left Iran before you had roots here. You were so young. You've even learned their language so well that it's hard for you to speak your mother tongue any more."

She stopped for a while. I looked at her and started to notice my sister without the apathy that had been dominating her personality of late. She was almost arguing with me.

"You left to get as far away from here as you could. It was always your dream. My dream was to stay here and fight. I wanted to make this a better place for people. I wanted to bring democracy, equality, and happiness to the people of this nation. I can't leave now, just because I've failed."

"Why do you say you've failed?"

"I have failed in everything I have attempted. It started with my being fired from the university. From there my life has gone nowhere, because there is nowhere for it to go after my career. I've failed in my marriage. I've been a poor mother, and a useless one. What's left?"

"You're one of the finest doctors in this country. Even now, they have to admit that. You came from a poor family, and look at you now. What you've done is incredible."

"I chose the wrong specialty," she said.

I wondered if she heard anything I said.

"I should have remained a pediatrician. These people don't understand what a psychiatrist is. They misuse my capabilities."

"Homa, you've taught them how to apply your talents. You've been a pioneer of psychiatry here."

Once again, she started jumping from subject to subject.

"You wouldn't know it, but this is a wealthy nation. Not just in oil, but in culture and history. There are monuments from the time of Dariush and the Hakhamanid still standing. These were built in the fourth or fifth century B.C.E. If you go to Persepolis and visit the museum, you can see artifacts from the fifth and sixth millennium.

"Our ancestors protected these for us. We should protect them for future generations. When I walk on the streets of New York, I feel like a stranger."

"Who doesn't?" I interrupted. She didn't appreciate the humor.

"But when I walk through the *koochehs* of Iran, I know I am at home. We have the Damavand Peak in Tehran, the tombs of Sadi and Hafez in Shiraz, the deserts of Systan, the oil wells of Khosestan, and the tea fields of Gilan.

"I feel safe in these places. Do you remember what our father taught us about the four pillars of nationality? They were culture, language, race, and religion. I have all of them here in Iran. What do I have in America?"

I couldn't answer that question. "Homa, you're being too idealistic. Look around. Look at the two of us, out in this warm weather dressed like good Moslem women. Look what this country has done to you. They took away your highest passion. It's like one pillar of your nationality is wiping out the other three. This is not our culture. This religion stems from Arabs, not Persians."

"That is true," she conceded. "But this is temporary. As a culture, we have survived thousands of years. For twenty-five hundred of those, we were dominated by monarchy. Still, Persians are survivors. They will survive this also."

"You call this surviving?! Before Islam, there were five empires in the world: the Persian, Egyptian, Chinese, Roman, and Greek. Look at those regions today. Persia and Egypt are far behind the other three in terms of advancement. The Islamic world has been hindered by its religious fundamentalism.

"Iran has been crippled since the seventh century, when Islam came. Now, revolutionaries have brought Khomeini and taken us back to those times."

"We made a mistake."

"It's not your fault! You were one of millions that supported the so-called imam."

"I should have known better. I was educated." Homa's tone of voice was tightening.

"It makes no difference." I could feel the guilt in her words.

"I've committed a crime. I have destroyed what I loved dearly."

"Stop it. It wasn't your fault."

"Then whose?"

"What about the 98 percent of the population that voted the Islamic Republic to power?"

"That's not what happened!"

"What do you mean? It was April 1, 1979, the first day of the government of God. I always remember the date because it's April Fool's Day in America."

"It didn't happen that way! The government was supposed to issue two different ballot sheets, one green and one red. The red did not support the proposal, while the green did. The red ballots, however, were almost impossible to find. The Revolutionary Guards would not give them out."

"Really?" I asked.

My ignorance of the subject encouraged her to be more assertive. "The vote reflected the people's desire to end the Pahlavi monarchy. In 1979, if you asked people if they wanted a shah or a republic, they would have chosen the republic.

"You also have to remember that most of the monarchy's defenders left Iran when the Shah did, and many of those who didn't were executed. In three months in 1979, one hundred thousand Iranians fled. It was an exodus."

"The ethnic cleansing that goes on in this society is awful," I said.

"As a nation, we are wealthy in terms of how many ayatollahs there are running around. Yet, we're short of professors. The Ayatollah Kani once said, 'we must purify our society in order to renew it.' They kill innocent people to purify the society." Homa's voice cracked as she spoke, but she acted as if none of the government's atrocities surprised her. She knew what suppressive governments were capable of.

"They do it in Bosnia now, too," she continued, "only it's Moslems that suffer there. Of course, the Islamic Republic is enraged by that war. They call it barbarism. But when they do it to other religious groups here, it's justified in the name of God. Killing is always wrong."

"You know, Homa, I have one question. I've never understood how the revolutionary government got Iran's educated, working women to accept the rules of *hijab*. Did the majority of them want to be covered this way from head to toe?"

"I don't think so. It started as a symbol. It was a symbol of the people's struggle against imperialism and corruption. It was like a uniform. By wearing it, you were making a statement against the pro-Western regime of Pahlavi."

"They did it by choice?" I couldn't believe it.

"Yes. It started in the universities. Female students started wearing scarves over their heads. Then, in 1980, Khomeini declared that women no longer had the right 'to be present in the governmental administration "naked." They may carry on their tasks, provided they use Islamic dress.'"

"And the women accepted it, just like that?"

"Of course not! They launched campaigns in the major cities of the country and Khomeini gave in. But then, the following year, wearing the Islamic outfit in government offices became mandatory again. Once again, people protested. But this time, the movement went nowhere because the Islamic Republic was well established and they had complete control of the media.

"They also had the Revolutionary Council, of course. They threatened women who ignored the rules of *hijab* with dismissal. Then, the ministry of education specified the color and the style of clothing to be worn by female students. These were black cloaks that covered girls as young as six, from head to toe."

"Did the men help at all?" I asked.

"Some did. Most of them didn't care, though. Just like they do in other parts of the world, they thought if women were forced out of the job market, there would be less unemployment."

"But Homa, these are the thoughts of ignorant men. What about all the forward thinking ones?"

"The forward thinkers, the ones that remember what Iran used to be, fought for women. They don't like living in these conditions. But most of them have fled to other countries."

"What about people like Mohsen?"

She paused before speaking. "I don't think he minds. I think he likes the perks. He likes being a part of the brotherhood men enjoy in Iran."

"Still, I can't understand why people would put up with these conditions."

"What else can they do? Besides, most people didn't foresee what we have today in Iran. They never thought it was that big an issue to force women to wrap a loose scarf casually over their head. At that time, no one talked about flogging, beating, and stoning. The disciplinary measures all came later."

"And Khomeini achieved his lifelong vendetta against Reza Shah." I added.

"True. Reza Shah removed the *hijab* cover by force and Khomeini brought it back by force."

"But Homa, you have to be selfish once in a while. What about you? You deserve a better life."

She smirked a bit. "No. I've given my life up to chase a lie."

"I want you to come with me. You can start again."

"I can't." She looked out across the park. "My wings have been broken for a long time. It's too late for me to try and fly." Then she smirked again and raised her arms a little. "These weak limbs couldn't hold a butterfly in the air. They're useless. I am useless."

We sat alone for a while and watched the families pass by. It was a peaceful morning in the park. You could not hear the sounds of people rushing around the city in their cars. I heard my sister mumbling the poem about the caged bird.

"Homa, look who's here." I saw our uncle coming toward us. "Hossain, what are you doing here? Come sit with us," I said.

"I'm looking for Homa." He stood before us, but he wouldn't sit down.

"What is the problem?" Homa asked.

"They've arrested Azar, Mr. Homayoun's youngest daughter, for violating the rules of *hijab*. She's going to be given 150 lashes unless Homa shows up in the court to testify that the girl is insane. We have to help her."

"What did she do?" I asked, surprised. Mr. Homayoun was a friend of Uncle Hossain.

"Nothing," my uncle looked at me like I'd asked a stupid question. Then, I think he remembered that I lived in the United States. "She's about sixteen and she put on some makeup. She was picked up by the Revolutionary Guards."

"One hundred fifty lashes for wearing a little lipstick? That's unbelievable!"

He ignored my comment and kept his attention on my sister. "Homa, you've got to help her."

"You know I don't like to do this," she said. "It is better for her to take the punishment than to be marked as insane for the rest of her life. The scars will heal."

"Homa, please, these people are friends of mine!"

"I don't think it's right."

"Her parents are desperate. They don't want the girl to be beaten. They think she won't be able to handle the pain. It could kill her." He was speaking frantically. "You have to come with me, Homa!"

Homa sat still for a while, and then she hung her head and gave in. "Let's go," she said.

They left. I walked back up the hill to Mother's house. I understood why Homa hated being who she was. As a pediatrician, they wouldn't call on her for those things.

The young girl was in a mire and Homa knew it. It's true, the beating may be too much for her and she may lose her life because of it. But being labeled insane has its own dire consequences. That girl would never be able to find a satisfying job or a husband for the rest of her life. She couldn't start a family, and she would be rejected by society.

Homa struggled with these dilemmas every day while she operated her private practice. Parents would plead with Homa to save their children. They knew that Homa was sympathetic enough to help them. Still, Homa never felt comfortable condemning the children. She knew that she was probably saving their lives because many children cannot survive the punishment of a severe flogging. However, she questioned if the lives were worth saving once they were burdened with the stigma of being declared insane.

I know she constantly worried for the children she'd done this for. She felt responsible for whatever became of their lives. The guilt she lived with was tremendous.

Chapter 27

The Doors Are Closing

I left Iran with Aunt Maryam, and without Homa, six days after my arrival. In Maryland, she helped us pack our belongings and prepare for our move back to California.

The two of us decided to drive across the United States together and take in some of the sights. On our way, a snowstorm forced us to stop for the night in a small town on the Oklahoma side of the Texas border.

Maryam and I spent a lot of our time talking about Homa and what we could do for her. That night, though, she told me about a chemotherapy clinic Mohsen had recently opened.

"Mohsen set up this clinic without ever asking for Homa's consent. It upset Homa, because she felt that he already worked too much. She was right."

"What do you mean?" I asked.

"The clinic needed to have a physician present at all times. But *Mohsen*'s schedule was too hectic. So, he had Homa watch the place every morning while he did his daily hospital rounds. I started bringing her there every morning at eight."

"What did you do all day in the clinic?" I asked.

"Nothing. We talked a little. I peeled apples and oranges for

Homa. The nurses brought tea. Most of the time, Homa just sat there and stared at the walls. She was miserable.

"She worried a lot, too," Maryam continued, "She was afraid someone from the ministry of health would come for an inspection and shut the operation down. She also hated the sight of all the cancer patients who were there for therapy."

"It must have been depressing to be surrounded by so many people with so little hope."

"It still is for her. And what makes it worse is that she can't help them. She has no expertise in the field. The whole experience is taking quite a toll on her."

"She works in the morning and then goes to her private practice every night?" I asked.

"No," she replied. "She closed her practice last summer."

"What?!" Sometimes I feel like I'm always the last person to know anything that goes on in my family. "Why did she do that?"

"She was getting harassed by the Revolutionary Guards."

"How?"

"Sometimes they would make appointments with her and bring their children as patients. During the consultation, they would complain to her for not complying with the *hijab*. They would accuse her of not wearing proper clothing and not covering her hair completely."

"That's terrible."

"Then they would complain about her fees. They said she charged more than the government permitted."

"What do you mean?"

"The government requires that Homa charge three hundred tuman for every half hour of service. In the meetings, the guards would waste an hour complaining about her clothing, and then they would refuse to pay for the total time. They felt like the time they spent complaining should be free."

"Really." I could feel my sister's frustration just by hearing the story. Three hundred tuman won't even buy a nice dinner in Iran.

"One time, they reported her and her office was closed down temporarily. They even placed a sign on the door that read: 'The doctor's office has been shut down because of the doctor's noncompliance with the rules of *hijab*.'

"That, more than anything, ruined her practice. People were afraid to see her after that. She started losing money. Soon, she couldn't cover her expenses. With the reduction of clients, Homa started working three days each week. Then it was two days, and then she just gave up."

Later on the trip, Maryam brought up another issue. "You know," she said, "I feel terrible leaving Homa like this. I have only one son, though, and I want to take care of him."

"What happened to Hamid?" I asked. "I thought he had a good job in Iran. Hossain told me his boss loved him. What made him give it all up?"

Maryam started crying. "His company wanted to display their products at a convention. Hamid was one of the company reps sent for the show. A woman there started talking with him about the display. I'm not sure if she was interested in any of the parts or if she just wanted to talk to a young man.

"Regardless, he handed her one of the company's business cards and asked her to call the office if she needed more information. It was a blank business card," she cried. "It didn't even have his name on it.

"I guess the woman's husband saw that and thought Hamid was making a pass at his wife. He called the Revolutionary Guards and they started beating him, right there, on the convention floor.

"They beat him up and took him to their office to beat him more. They finally released him that night. He came home with his face so swollen and bruised that I couldn't recognize him. That was it for him. He couldn't stay after that. He left Iran as soon as he recovered."

"He never told me. I was surprised. Thank God they didn't kill him."

"Strange, no matter what happens to our family in Iran, we always have to thank God that things aren't worse," she said.

By this time, we had managed to pass through Texas and were approaching Albuquerque, New Mexico. Another storm was in front of us. We needed to find a motel to spend the night. The snow was heavy and the road was closed.

That night, Maryam and I had dinner at the coffee shop in the motel. We went to the bar for a drink afterward. I was tired from having driven for so long. Maryam looked tired, too. It was nice to be with her, though. When Homa and I were young, she had been a second mother to us. As we got older, we developed a great friendship.

I watched Maryam as she sat across from me in the lounge. She was watching the television behind me. There was a hockey game on TV. I looked at her face. She had incredible green eyes. I looked at the deep etches that came down on either side of her mouth. It made me think about what a tough life she was having. It must be strange for her to be in America.

She looked at me after a while and said, "I wish Homa had come with us."

"We would have had a lot of fun together," I admitted.

The road did not open until eleven the next morning. We hadn't driven more than five miles when Maryam again started talking about Homa.

"Parvin, my heart stops when I think about the shock therapy they put Homa through."

"What therapy?" I never knew.

"Her doctor prescribed it. Homa, though, insisted she didn't need it. She always told them she didn't need the therapy. She used to scream, 'There's nothing wrong with me, except that I've screwed up my life!' I had to take her there."

"What happened? Did it hurt her? Did it help?"

"It didn't help her. I don't think it hurt. I hope it didn't."

We drove for a while in silence. I was afraid of what shock therapy might have done to my sister's memory. She used to place great value on her mind.

I remember being in an accident with my sister once in Tehran. We were on our way to a party. She was crossing an intersection when the driver next to her, in the far left lane, decided to cut her off. He turned right onto the road they were crossing. We collided, but were not hurt because both cars were moving slowly. Homa got out of the car and looked at the other driver.

"Now where on earth are you allowed to make a right turn from the left lane?" she asked him.

"I'm sorry," he replied, "I tried to pass you, but I guess I didn't try hard enough."

When we started driving again, Homa said a curious thing to me. "I am glad that was a minor accident," she said. "Can you imagine what a waste it would be if I was to get killed in an auto accident? All these years of studying and accumulating knowledge about people and their brains would be wasted."

As I thought about it, I remembered that my sister was rarely seen without a new book she was reading to learn something.

"I guess Homa never thought all her knowledge would be put at risk because her hair and her beautiful eyes offended a *mullah*."

"No," Maryam continued. "The doctor arranged the sessions for nine o'clock at night, right after he closed his office. He conducted the procedure himself. Mohsen would pick her up after the session to take her home. Then he would want her at the clinic the next morning."

"How could he be so demanding?!"

"I've never had an answer for that. I've cried many times when I've thought about how much Homa craved her husband's affection and how indifferent he was to her."

"She always loved him."

"I know. After her experience with Keyvan, Mohsen was the only man in Homa's life."

"I just wonder if she was the only woman in his life," I said.

Chapter 28

The Attempt to Escape

In the summer of 1993, I sent my son to Tehran to gain experience working with some of my associates in the city. It was during that summer that Homa's world crumbled. One morning, while my husband Reiner and I were working, Romin called us from my mother's home.

"Hello?" I answered the phone.

"Hi, Mom, it's me. Listen, I have bad news."

"What? What is it?"

"Now, I don't want you to get scared, but I have to tell you that something awful just happened. Your sister's in Arad Hospital. She's in a coma, but they say she'll be okay in a few days."

"Jesus! What happened?" I was instantly frantic.

"It looks like she tried to commit suicide," he said.

Then I couldn't speak. I just cried loudly on the line. When I gained my composure, I asked more questions. I flooded him with questions as I howled into the receiver. "How did this happen? Where are you? Where's your grandmother?"

"Grandma's at the hospital. Apparently, Aunt Homa bought a bunch of tranquilizers and took them during the afternoon, earlier today. I guess Khadijeh, her maid, was with her at home. She said

Homa was restless and wouldn't stop pacing up and down the floors. She was taking the tranquilizers to calm down. Anyway, I guess she took a lot of them because she collapsed and became unconscious fairly quickly. Khadijeh said she heard Homa call her from one of the bedrooms, but by the time she found her she was already unconscious.

I was here, talking with your mother in the dining room. The phone rang and I guess it was Khadijeh. Anyway, Grandma started panicking. I was afraid she might have a nervous breakdown. She was raving and reaching for the phone, but I could not understand most of what she screamed. When she tried to dial, her fingers shook wildly. She could not seem to remember the number she wanted to call. She wanted to call my aunt's doctor, but as she shouted the numbers her fingers did not respond.

"That's all I know right now, I'll call you again when I know more," he said.

After the call, I just sat in my office, motionless. I didn't know what I could do except pray for Homa to regain consciousness. I was planning a trip to Iran in about a month and I prayed that my sister would hang on long enough for me to see her. I wanted one more chance to convince her to come back with me.

Reiner and I arrived in Tehran in August. We took a taxi with my son to see Homa at the hospital the first morning I was there. I knew that she had come out of her coma after three days, but I still had little information about her condition. I asked Romin to explain what had happened in the past few weeks.

"While she was in a coma, we watched her every day. I came to the hospital after work with Hossain and waited by her side for her to wake up. I would grab her wrist, stare at her lifeless face, and visualize her coming to. I would imagine her wrist moving or her eyes fluttering, but nothing happened."

"Was anyone with you?" I asked.

"Yes," he said, "there were always people present, but they handled the situation in different ways. Some sat at her bedside weeping in disbelief. Others stood an arm's-length away with their eyes lowered, like they were shedding pity. I was the only one touching her. I kneeled before her, and put her stiff hand in mine and kissed her softly.

"When the doctors surrounded her and stuffed tubes through a hole they'd made in her neck to drain off the liquid that had collected in her lungs, I stood next to her. Her entire body arched in a painful reflex. I still remember her face flushing red and grimacing in awful pain as if she was being beaten."

"I was crying in the taxicab as we drove home."

"When she woke up, it was a great relief. Of course, she still couldn't speak. It was obvious that she didn't know where she was or how she had gotten there. I was worried. She wasn't really awake yet. I was afraid that in a few days when she realized what was going on, she would be lost again.

"From then on, it was no longer a matter of focusing. I had to spend my time with Homa talking and listening. I tried to make her feel guilty. I tried to make her realize that people needed her to live. I was frustrated, though. Aunt Homa lived with constant pain, and the pain was so great that she opted for the ultimate sacrifice to evade it. What could I say to alleviate that?"

"Nothing," I said, as I blew my nose. "You can't say anything. I can't help her either. She needs professionals."

"Those next few days were really rough for her. She had very little energy. They wouldn't let her eat. For nine days she lived on sugar and water fed through an IV. I guess they would occasionally inject blended meals through a tube stuffed in one of her nostrils, but that was it."

We were driving through the city now. The traffic was very heavy. I thought about all the noise that must surround the hospital.

"Does she ever leave the hospital?" I asked.

"We took her out once to Karim's villa, on Friday." He looked at me and continued, "The men and women sat on different sides of the balcony outside. Homa was sitting with two ladies. They were both covered by Islamic chadors. I could tell that she was bored.

"I didn't like seeing her there. There was nothing for her. Her husband and his brothers sat and talked for hours. I don't know if Mohsen even cared that his wife sat nervously across the way trying to pass the time until she could be alone again."

"Was she really silent?" I asked.

"I wouldn't let her be. I bothered her. I stayed with her all day and kept talking to her, even though she wasn't very responsive."

"Good."

"The day before we took her out, we went to a park with her private nurse and let her walk for a while. She didn't really walk. She paced. Before we left the hospital, she paced again. I was with her. We were waiting for the nurse. She was walking stiffly up and down the hall with her shoulders barely moving.

"At one point, I grabbed her by the arm and urged her to loosen up. I didn't understand why she could be so stiff, and then she told me.

" 'I'm nervous' she whispered. She could not speak yet.

" 'Why are you nervous?' I asked.

"She said, 'Wouldn't you be nervous if you were in my position?'

"I think it was humiliating for her to have friends and family around her when she was still recovering."

We pulled into a parking spot across from the hospital. I took a deep breath and wiped my face as we walked up the stairway in front of the hospital's main entrance.

When we saw Homa, she looked pale. She was still unable to talk well. She had a private room at the hospital which her husband had arranged for.

It was a small room with a bed, and a couch for visitors. Vases filled with flowers were placed throughout the room. The flowers came from friends and family, but none of them were from her husband.

A nurse was with her constantly. Three of them rotated shifts around-the-clock. The conversations in the hospital were very limited. She couldn't talk much and she felt humiliated by the circumstances.

On another afternoon, when we were visiting, a family came to the room and asked to see her. They said they'd brought their son all the way from Ahvaz, a city in southwest Iran. The physician there could not diagnose the boy's problem. He sent them to Tehran to find Dr. Homa Darabi. The physician said she would be the only doctor in Iran who could correctly diagnose the child.

The family first went to Homa's office in Tehran. They found it empty. By asking around, they had discovered that Homa was hospitalized at Arad Hospital. Homa agreed to see them, and ended up spending about two hours with the family in her hospital room.

She discovered that the boy's problem was a physical one and that it was treatable. She referred the family to a colleague of hers, confident that the boy's problem could be resolved.

The parents were ecstatic. They wanted to repay Homa by giving her all the money they had with them. She refused to accept it. She told them she only helped the boy because they traveled so far for him and she felt guilty. She was lying, of course.

It was amazing to watch my sister with these people. I'd come in the morning to spend some time with her, and her mood was just awful. She just lay in her hospital bed, moping. All she could talk about was how miserable she was.

Once she started working with this family, though, something came over her. Her instincts seemed to take over. She became a doctor again. A complete metamorphosis occurred right before my eyes. While they were there, she was efficient and professional. In fact, she was almost upbeat. Watching her work with a patient was like watching an artist at her canvas.

Sadly, though, she returned to her isolated state when the family left. Again, she talked of her uselessness and her doom.

Within a few days after our arrival, she was discharged and allowed to go home. In the mornings, now, Mohsen brought her to Mother's house to be with us. At night, he came again to take her home.

I came home from some meetings downtown one afternoon and Homa became curious about what my husband and I were trying to do in Iran. Reiner was still downtown trying to extend his visa.

"Parvin, what did you do today?" Homa asked.

"This morning, we had a meeting with some representatives from the Civil Aviation Administration," I said.

"What for?" she asked.

"We were discussing some of their plans for the new airport they want to build in Tehran."

"How was the meeting?"

"It was fine," I said. "You want to hear something funny?"

"Sure," she said.

"Well, this airport was originally going to be built during the shah's regime, but after the revolution, construction ceased. So, the representative we're meeting with starts off by giving a short presentation to our group. In the middle of his introduction, he says, 'The plans for this operation were originally developed under the guidance of the previous regime. Unfortunately, the revolution started. I beg your pardon, fortunately, the revolution started and we had to delay the program for fifteen years.' "

"We all looked at each other and didn't know what to say. How can it be fortunate that a program was delayed by fifteen years?'"

Homa was smiling.

"My gosh, Homa, we didn't know what to do. We all sat there and tried to control our laughter in front of the officials that were with us. The speaker was completely embarrassed. He stuttered through the rest of his presentation as if he knew he'd made an awful mistake in front of his peers."

"He's right," Homa said. "Most of the technology in the country predates the revolution. Nothing's really been done since then. We can attribute part of that to the Iran-Iraq war that went on for so long."

"Eight years," I agreed.

"The war cost this nation in countless ways. Young men came back permanently injured, chemical warfare left millions sick, and the whole thing was based on a vendetta Khomeini had against Saddam Hussain."

Homa was starting to revel in the topic. "He gave the children he sent off to war a plastic key to hang around their neck. Khomeini said it was the key to heaven and told them to use it if they died. I don't think we can ever forgive ourselves for following such a leader."

"Homa, you've got to stop blaming yourself. Saddam Hussain attacked Iran and the military was forced to defend their country. Don't make it any bigger than that."

"But if we didn't have the revolution, there would have been no vendetta and no attack."

"You don't know that."

"You just can't appreciate what this war has done to the people of Iran. I've seen too many young adults mentally destroyed by this war. Bombing raids used to be a constant worry for people in Tehran. It was like the entire population had put their lives in a lottery. All we could do was pray."

"You're right. I can't appreciate that fear. How did you manage?"

"We were lucky to have the *dakhmeh*. It was the closest thing to a bomb shelter that one could live in. We felt safe two stories underground. In fact, a lot of our family used to spend nights with us.

"We'd be at the dinner table and sirens would go off in the city warning people of a coming raid. The lights would go out, too, of course. Then we would all gather in one of the bedrooms and wait out the storm together. It was pretty frightening, because you could hear the sound of bombs exploding in other parts of the city. It was a horrible war that crippled this nation. But we were lucky. "

"Well, the war is over now. The country is trying to rebuild."

"Things aren't getting any better. People still don't have enough money on which to live. The economy is in awful shape, and there's not enough incentive for people to work. But whenever people start to complain about these conditions, the government reacts by arresting women for failing to comply with religious rules. This distracts people from the real issues. It's disturbing to even think about."

"Homa, why don't you come back with us to America? We'll be leaving next Tuesday morning. Please, Homa, come with us."

"I can't. I have nothing to do in America. I have no money, no way of getting there, and I have no clothes to wear."

"You don't need any of those things. We'll get you a ticket. The two of us can go on a shopping spree once we arrive in San Francisco."

"I have nothing to wear on the plane."

"What?" I asked, surprised. "What's wrong with what you're wearing now?" She had a dark blue warm-up suit on.

"No. I can't go in this."

I never remembered Homa wearing dark colors by choice. Most Iranian women, on the other hand, wear black for most occasions. If you go to a gathering of Iranians, probably 90 percent of the women present will be dressed in black. Red is a color which usually only young children wear.

Homa loved bright colors. To see her in Iran with such a dark gym suit was odd.

"No," she insisted again, "I can't go to America. I don't want to discuss it anymore. I have to stay here."

"Homa! Please come with us. This country cannot appreciate people like you. Think about your health. We don't want to see you like this anymore."

"I told you, I have no clothes to wear."

"But that can't be an excuse! What about your grandson, Azita's new baby? Don't you want to see him?"

"I can't go and visit my grandson the way I am. I need better clothes."

"Homa! Come on, now. We'll buy you all the clothes you need. We'll spend a day in Union Square, in the heart of San Francisco, and the two of us can find a beauty shop and have our hair done. Then you can leave for a week and visit your daughter and her family in Montreal. Just come with me," I pleaded.

Before she could answer, Reiner opened the front door and came in the room. He was visibly upset and Homa turned to him. "Reiner, what's the problem?"

"They wouldn't extend my visa. I have to leave Iran on Monday night, before midnight."

"Really? That's a pity," she said in a flat voice.

Homa had changed the subject, and she was glad. "We'll go tomorrow, and rearrange your travel plans," I suggested.

The night Reiner was to leave, we arranged a get-together at my mother's home for some of our family. Homa came over in the morning and spent the day with us, as she had been doing all week. But just before the guests started arriving, she left.

I tried to make her stay, but she refused. She wasn't prepared to be seen by relatives.

Chapter 29

At the Abyss

The last time I saw my sister was in November 1993, when I stopped in Iran while traveling to an air show in Dubai. I had two days to spend in Iran before my flight left to cross the Persian Gulf. I was to spend four days in Dubai before returning to Iran for two more days and finally returning to California.

I wanted to see Homa and try once more to get her to leave Iran. I wasn't optimistic, though. I knew the best chance I had had come one year earlier, when I fought with her husband about the issue.

The two of us met at our mother's home and spent the afternoon together. I was immediately distressed when I saw her. Her condition had deteriorated dramatically over the last three months.

All she wore was a dark gym suit which she covered with a coat and scarf when she went outside. Her face was pale, as if she hadn't been in the sun for a while, and she used no makeup. Her expression was frozen. She had a look of indifference that never faded.

I wasn't confident that I would change her mind.

Once again, I asked, "Homa, please, Reiner and I are living in Truckee, California, now. It's a beautiful place in the mountains, close to Lake Tahoe. We can take care of you there. You'll be surrounded by tranquillity in that environment."

And once again she rejected the idea. "I belong here. America is no place for me."

"Just think about it," I said, frustrated. "I leave tomorrow for Dubai, but when I return in five days we can leave together."

"I have nothing to wear."

"Come with me to Dubai, then. We can buy everything you want there. I promise."

"That's not the problem. Nothing fits me anymore. Mohsen brought me some outfits from Frankfurt, but they were all twice my size. They were ugly, too. He bought junk."

"They would have been a closer fit on me, than her." Our mother could hear us from the kitchen.

"Homa, please."

"I'll think about it."

Five days later, I returned. Homa spent the evening with me at our mother's. Mom asked the two of us to go in the living room and spend time with each other while she prepared dinner in the kitchen. I was shocked by her request, because it marked the first time she had ever intentionally given my sister and me time to be alone together.

"What's on your mind, Mom?" I asked her.

"Parvin, talk to her. Get her to change her mind. Her American passport has been renewed, and she won't have any difficulty getting to the United States now."

"What about her husband?" I asked "Will he let her go?"

"He said we can do whatever we please with her."

"But do you have his written permission?"

"No. But he says—"

"It doesn't matter what he says. He rarely means the things he says. You have to get it from him in writing. When I was here in August, I met with an attorney and he told me there was nothing we could do unless her husband gave his consent in writing."

"You just talk to your sister. I'll take care of getting permission from her husband."

She talked as if she had some covert plan to get what she wanted from Mohsen. She didn't though, and I knew it. Still, there was nothing I could even try doing without Homa's consent, and so I continued pestering her about the trip.

"Homa, why do you want to stay here?"

"What can I do in America? I have no capabilities, Parvin."

"What do you mean? You are a doctor—a child psychiatrist."

"No. I *used* to be a doctor. I lost my job, and I lost my practice, and now I have no skills. I've been without work for too long. It would be impossible to start again."

"You can't forget your profession. It's like riding a bicycle: once you learn, you never forget. I've seen you work. I know you have the capabilities. You could be one of the finest doctors in America."

"It's just not my profession."

"What, then?"

"I am such a helpless person. I have no capabilities. All I do all day is sit and eat when people put food in front of me. I don't know how to do anything. My situation is hopeless. I have no money."

I could feel my heart sink as she said these words to me. Listening to her, I felt as though I might see the life spilling out of her if I looked to the ground. I had to change the subject.

"You have a new home, now. You left the *dahkmeh* right?"

"Yes, Mohsen bought a home from his brother in the hills."

"Are you going to decorate it? It might be a good project for you. Why don't you spend some time decorating the place?"

"It is not my home. I didn't chose it. He bought it without talking to me. He'll buy the furnishings that way, too. If I tried to get involved, he wouldn't let me, not in the state I'm in. I am helpless."

"Why don't you just leave him and come to America and start a new life?"

"I told you, I can't."

Still stubborn, I thought.

"I should die." Homa looked at the floor.

"What?"

"I don't want to live anymore. All I do is eat and wear out clothes. I've caused enough hardship."

"You can't talk like this," I pleaded, "Fight back. You're ill. Come with me and we'll fight it together."

"I can't leave. I love this country and I need to die here. There's nothing wrong with me, either. I am a perfectly sane woman who has messed up her life. Now I am hopeless."

Our mother came out of the kitchen. "Mohsen is here to take Homa home," she announced.

I watched Homa get up from her chair and wrap her long coat around her shaking body. She said good-bye to me and promised to see me one more time before I left the next night.

After Homa left, I talked with our mother for a while. "I'm worried, Mom. She needs help. We have to do something."

"I don't know what we can do. I'm just as worried. We need her husband or at least her children to feel like we do, but they don't. They won't help her."

"Talk to Mohsen. Ask him to put Homa in a hospital. She needs to be watched."

"Her doctor has ordered thirty more electroshock sessions. They start tomorrow night."

"It doesn't help! Why can't we talk to her children and tell them the truth about their mother?"

"Mohsen would raise hell. He doesn't want his daughters to worry about her. Besides, how can you let people know that a doctor has gone insane?"

"She hasn't gone insane! She's depressed. It's a disease. We have to find a way to treat it."

"It's Mohsen she needs. But he won't help—he doesn't even come with me to take her for therapy."

The next evening Homa came over and we spent some time together. Our conversation was light. We didn't talk about anything confrontational. I refrained from begging her to come back with me. Mostly, we spent a lot of time sitting together in silence.

Uncle Hossain came at nine to transport Homa to her doctor for therapy. Afterward, he planned to return and take me to the airport.

I held my sister tightly and kissed her cheek. Tears were pouring from my eyes. I knew she had a rough year ahead of her. I knew I couldn't be near her to help her through it.

My sister considered herself to be the helpless one, but I can't recall being more useless in my lifetime. There was nothing I could do to bring her out of the dark. She left that night, and I waited for Hossain to return.

Later, as I rode with Hossain to the airport, I asked him about Homa's session earlier that night.

"It was pitiful," he said. "Mohsen came late and the doctor had to perform the electroshock therapy without him."

"It doesn't surprise me," I said.

"She needs him, you know. He's the only one she can have intelligent discussions with. But he spends too much of his time away from her."

As my plane rushed down the runway, I felt the thrust pulling me into the seat. I looked out of the window and saw the lights from the city spread out below me. I knew I wouldn't be back for a long time.

Chapter 30

February 12, 1994

"Hi, Homa, it's Parvin. I'm calling from San Francisco. It's Romin's twenty-first birthday and we came down to the city to celebrate with him."

"Oh" she said in the same dry voice that seemed to have overcome her two years earlier. "That is nice. We called him yesterday to wish him the best, but he wasn't home."

I gave the phone to Romin. He talked with her for a few minutes. When I got the phone back, our mother was on the line.

"Parvin, you'll never believe what your sister did."

"What?"

"She went through their medical book library, hundreds of them, and pulled out all of hers."

"Why?"

"She had them all thrown away. She said she didn't need them."

"Oh my God."

"By the time Mohsen realized the books were missing, the trash bin had been emptied."

"I can't believe it's getting this bad."

"I know," she said. "Did you talk with her daughters?"

"I don't think they want to hear from me, but I wrote a letter to Azita and sent it registered to Canada. I haven't received an answer."

"What did you say in the letter?"

"Basically, I told her that I didn't know anything about her relationship with her mother, but Homa needs help. I asked her to go to Tehran with her sister and bring Homa back with them.

"I also told her not to worry about money. I said we would sell your house to pay for it, like we planned."

"I think I heard about your letter. She called Mohsen a while ago and he told her you didn't know what you were talking about. He said there was nothing wrong with Homa and that she shouldn't be worried."

"Why didn't you say something? You could have told them the truth."

"I am not sure they want to know the truth," she said.

"What's the use then? Where is she now?"

"She is in the other room. I'll get her on the phone."

I heard Homa take the phone. "Homa, why don't you come to California in June for Romin's graduation?"

"I can't. I have nothing to wear."

"This again? We don't want your clothes, we want *you*. Whatever you want, we can buy here. Remember when I came to your daughter's graduation? I think you should come to your nephew's now. He's getting his bachelor's."

"I don't know. Let me think about it."

"What is there to think about?"

"I have to think about it. Now, your phone bill is getting too high. Tell Romin I wish him the best and give my regards to your husband."

I hung up the phone and talked about the conversation with my husband.

"Did you tell your mother what you wrote in the letter?"

"No, not everything. I didn't tell her that I wrote about the possibility of Homa taking her own life if she is left in Tehran."

"It's for the best, I guess. It's strange, children today don't seem to want to have anything to do with their parents once they become financially independent."

I listened to Reiner speak, but my mind was thinking about something else. "Reiner," I said, "this isn't good. If she got rid of all those books, she must be reaching the end."

I didn't sleep that night.

February 20, 1994, Tehran

Hossain went to his office in the morning and found a fax I had sent him overnight.

> Dear Uncle Hossain,
>
> Please purchase two tickets from Lufthansa Airlines and tell Homa you want to take her on a shopping spree in San Francisco. Get her on the plane and bring her here.
>
> With love,
>
> Parvin

Two days later, I woke up to the sound of my uncle's voice, heartbroken as he told me the details of my sister's tragic death.

Epilogue

Four days after I found out about Homa, I was asked to fly to Los Angeles for an interview with an Iranian television program called *MA* (We). They wanted to know about my sister because they thought it was a story the Iranian people would want to hear.

It is an unsettling fact that when something like this happens, people tend to run from it. They avoid you. The sadness scares them and keeps them from wanting to be around you. I guess it's because you can't seem to stop crying. I hadn't been much of a conversationalist during the days following my sister's death, and I started to lose touch with the people around me.

But the media isn't that way. They want to know you when your life becomes tragic. They thrive on that kind of sadness. It was easy for me to agree to talk to them, because I needed to talk to someone who would listen. Of course, they were manipulating the story to suit their own needs, but they listened first.

Since the revolution in 1979, Iranians have found safe havens in countries like the United States, Germany, and France. They could not succeed in fighting the revolution from within Iran, so they left, or rather they fled, and started a quiet assault on the Islamic Republic from abroad.

Here, in the United States, Iranians are free to publish and to communicate to others their plight. In fact, several news organizations have developed throughout the country that address Iranian issues. Of course, each one of them has a slant and a reason for publishing material denouncing the government of their mother country.

One of these organizations is *MA*. I knew *MA* was more interested in the political aspects of my sister's death than they were in my grief. Still, I felt I should say something after what happened, so I agreed to talk with them.

In Los Angeles, I found the managing director of *MA* television. She drove straight to a studio in Orange County to interview me. There, I met an accomplished psychologist who remembered Homa because she herself was once a professor at the University of Tehran.

The three of us were seated around a table in a small studio. The host asked most of the questions. The psychologist was there to evaluate the situation from her point of view.

They asked me questions about my sister, her self-immolation, her education, her children, her husband, and her life. I explained everything I could, as well as I could, but some questions were tougher than others.

I didn't have any good answers to the tough questions. Mostly, they were the same questions I had been asking myself for years. I laid most of the blame on her husband. He always treated his wife like property.

The interview was very painful. I broke into tears several times when I tried to explain things. Anger and frustration were brewing inside me. I wanted vengeance. I remember wishing I could have some kind of magic wand that could change things.

When we were finished, the director of the station took me back to her home, to sleep and I left early the next day for San Jose.

On the flight north, I found myself sheltered from distractions in the airplane. I sat alone and looked out the window. I watched the Los

Angeles landscape pass under the plane as we gained altitude. I watched neighborhoods and office buildings and parks while they grew smaller and smaller. And then I couldn't see anything. The plane was swallowed by clouds and sheets of white mist were floating by the aircraft.

When we flew above the clouds, I no longer saw things as they were. The plane felt still. The sound of the engine was hollow and seemed silent. The sky around us was deep blue. I kept my eyes on the level deck of clouds that lay beneath us.

I felt isolated in the air and I felt a deep sense of regret for what had happened to my sister. There was also sorrow for what was happening to our family. In the face of pain, a family is supposed to pull together and regroup. But how could this one?

Having grown up with Homa made getting older pleasurable, because we could always share memories of being young. Once you grow up you can never be young again, and when someone dies you lose a part of yourself that will never come back.

Some blows are too tough to recover from. I knew that I would never look at my life as I did before. Things would be darker from now on. Even staring at a beautiful bed of white clouds, I could see torment in them. I wanted to jump. I wanted to leave the plane and dive into the clouds below.

I thought about giving up right then. *Walk away from life, like your sister!*

But I couldn't let myself think that way. It wasn't true. She didn't give up. It's not that simple. She died, and this family has got to come to terms with that. We've got to stop telling ourselves that it would be easier to understand if it had been something else. What if it was a car accident, or a heart attack? We'd still be shocked and sad, but we wouldn't be beaten. We'd come together and help each other and others would also help. There would be empathy and compassion.

It hasn't been like that, though. The family has fallen apart. Outside help has been hard to find. Homa's legacy is even argued about by us. Some see her as a powerful image of a protest. Others remember her as a weak woman who could not speak for herself. To them, her only self-made decision was her final act. Her death reaffirms their belief in her inferiority. That, I think, is what her husband would feel. The man couldn't even sit with his wife during the final hours of her life. I didn't want to think about him.

In San Jose, I had something else to do. Memorials in Iran are very long and dreadful under the guidelines of Shiite Islam. They begin with burial services at the grave on the first day after the death. The mourning then continues for the next forty days. In this period, the third, seventh, and the fortieth day are marked by formal gatherings. After the first forty days, the death is mourned annually, on the anniversary of the first day.

Somehow, I had to recreate a part of this process in the United States. My sister had many friends and relatives here and they would need a place to gather. I had never dreamed of coordinating such an observance and had no idea where to begin. I contacted the local Iranian newspaper, the *Khavaran*. It was the same paper I placed the announcement in the day Homa died. With their help, I arranged a service in San Jose and set the date for February 28, the seventh day.

At San Jose State University, the service was impressive. About two hundred people came to pay their respects. The ceremony was led by the publisher of the *Khavaran*. It involved various speakers, including myself.

The first speaker talked about the atrocities committed against women in Iran. He focused his words on the emotional toll educated women like my sister face when they try to live in Iran. It was a very good speech.

Still, I felt an uneasiness in the crowd. I knew they also struggled to find a rationale for what had happened. For them, it might have been a shorter search. Most of the audience never knew my sister. They could easily portray her in their minds as an unstable crackpot eager to draw attention to herself in a most dreadful way.

When I spoke, I focused on the accomplishments of her life so that people wouldn't make such quick judgments. I recited a synopsis of her career as a physician that described her work both in the United States and in Iran. I wanted people to see that she was a professional. She was one of the foremost psychiatrists in all of Iran.

It was a tough speech to give. I understood that many people were watching me. The audience was dominated by Iranian students from the university. What could they have thought of a woman who so hated her life as to terminate it?

I know what I would have thought at that age. I would have called it a waste. I would have said something like, "Oh, she must have been crazy." I would have thought she had a mental defect of some kind.

All these young people were sitting before me. They were looking for answers. I had none to give. To close, I followed the suggestion of an Iranian journalist who had sent a message that was read by the first speaker. I asked the audience to forego the traditional practice of allowing a moment of silence to respect the spirit of the dead. Instead, I asked them all to clap their hands loudly, and repeat my sister's last cry.

Death to tyranny!
Long live freedom!
Long live Iran!

It was a touching moment for me, because the people really screamed. I sensed a shared feeling of grief coupled with outrage. I was immediately driven to tears by the gesture, and so I quietly thanked everyone and returned to my seat.

It was also nice that I wasn't alone. My son was there and so were a few of my closest friends. After the service, some of the guests that knew Homa came with me to a friend's apartment in Sunnyvale for a small private gathering.

There, people talked about Homa and what they remembered about her. They talked about Iran and what they remembered about the country. A lot of them told stories about when and why they decided to leave. All of them had opinions on the political climate today. Mostly, though, people felt a sense of shame, that something like this could happen, and none of them had done anything to prevent it.

When I returned home the night after the service, I was alone because my husband had gone overseas for business. The inside of my house seemed especially empty, and I felt more alone than I ever had before.

My sister had always been a part of me. We did not need to be close to each other for me to feel her in my heart every day. A person I'd grown up with—someone that was always next to me—was lost forever.

I stood inside our doorway and stared across the empty living room. Moonlight was shining through the windows and dusting the furniture with its blue glow. The silence was deafening.

When the phone rang, I didn't recognize it right away. By the third ring, I realized that I had to get up to answer it. When I picked up the receiver I coughed out a muffled "Hello?"

The caller had an Iranian voice. He was calling from Paris. He wanted to ask me about my sister and her death. He wanted to know what I knew about the current status of women's rights in Iran.

I think he caught me at a bad moment. Maybe because I'd just awakened, I hadn't fully pulled myself together. In the past few days I'd been talking to a lot of people about my sister, and I'd always managed to approach the discussions with the right amount of political tact.

But this morning, on the phone, I went into a rage. My temper got the best of me, and I started cursing the establishment of Iran.

"The *mullahs* always tell their disciples that life on earth is merely a preparation for the afterlife, right? So why, then, can't they all go and kill themselves and leave the rest of us here to live on our own!

"Look at them! They are as scared of life on this earth as anyone. If what they're preaching is so divine, then why must they feel a need to enforce it at gunpoint? They're holding an entire nation hostage.

"And even worse, they haven't got the slightest clue of how to run a country. They stripped my sister of her ability to practice medicine. In a country with less than one doctor per thousands of citizens, they actually fired one for not covering her hair properly. Where is the logic in that?!"

I was on the phone with Paris for nearly a half-hour. I don't think they asked me more than three questions the whole time. I was well rested for the first time in a week, and I guess I had a lot to say. In the end, the caller asked me to meet with his organization in France and I agreed.

After the conversation, I went downstairs and started to brew some coffee. Before I could pour my first cup, the phone rang again. This time it was a group of Iranians in Canada. They called to offer their condolences and share some stories about loved ones they had lost in Iran through similar circumstances.

That day, I must have gotten a hundred calls from people all over the world. I listened to them tell me about atrocities committed against their relatives in the name of God by the Islamic Republic.

The calls continued for the entire day. I can't actually remember whether I found time for breakfast or lunch.

Later in the evening, the calls finally stopped for a little while and I found time to relax. It was an emotional afternoon, and I was exhausted from constantly talking to people about sad things. I had been crying for most of the day.

I poured a glass of red wine for myself, sat down in the living room, and tried to calm down. On that night, I no longer felt so alone. I was accompanied by the thoughts of all those people who had called to share my grief, and to relate their own. I started to sense a larger meaning to Homa's death.

When the phone rang again, I jumped a little. I felt as though I'd spilled my wine but when I checked the glass, it was resting steadily on my lap. A male voice was on the line. It was the owner of the Iranian radio station in Los Angeles.

"Dr. Darabi, my name is Mr. Morovati. You were interviewed by our station a few days ago. I would first like to thank you for that. I was very impressed with what you had to say."

"Thank you," I replied. I was surprised to hear from the owner of the station. I wondered why he was calling because I'd never met him before.

"I would like to hold a memorial wake in honor of your late sister. We are all deeply touched by the story of her struggle and the statement she made in her final moments. We would like to help her reach others. We are planning to gather on Sunday, the sixth of March. Do you think you could attend? It would mean a lot for us to have you there."

I was very grateful. "Of course, I would love to be there."

"Would you feel comfortable preparing a statement? If you could say a few things for our audience, they would greatly appreciate—"

"Of course. I wouldn't mind at all."

"We can pick you up at the airport, if you like. Perhaps we can even tape another interview in the morning. Oh, and I have one more favor to ask."

"What is it?"

"Would you be able to provide us with a large picture of your sister so that it can be placed on a wreath at the service?"

"Oh, no problem, I can easily do that. I'll have one made. I'll have to arrange an itinerary and then get back to you about the trip."

"Fine, then. I'll look forward to hearing from you."

The next few days brought even more calls from people wanting to offer me their condolences and invite me to various services. I found myself turning off the ringer at night so that I could sleep undisturbed. During the days, however, I spent almost all my time on the phone.

I never really understood how many supporters of women's rights operated around the world. I was amazed at the impact my sister's death had made on people.

Some things I learned were not as uplifting, however. Many of the groups that called to offer condolences seemed more interested in gaining my endorsement for their own causes. Staying ahead of these well-wishers became a difficult task.

A couple of days after making my commitment to go to Los Angeles, I made arrangements to make a similar trip to Oregon. I was asked by a gentleman by the name of Mr. Zar to speak at a gathering there. I agreed to do so. I also agreed to travel to the city of Portland after completing my commitment with Mr. Morovati and another commitment I'd made to a group called the National Council of Women for a Democratic Iran, in Washington, D.C.

A couple of days before leaving for Los Angeles, I got a call from an Iranian man who had apparently heard about my trip.

"May I speak with Mrs. Darabi?"

"This is she," I replied.

"Hello, Mrs. Darabi, I am calling you from Oregon. I would like to tell you how deeply sorry I am to hear about your most recent loss."

"Thank you, it's very nice of you to do so. I'm sorry, what was your name, sir? I've been talking with so many people these past few days, I must not have understood it."

He responded quickly. "I understand you're going to be speaking at a memorial service here in Oregon on March 13, the service coordinated by Mr. Zar. Is that correct?"

His question puzzled me. "Well, yes, I've made plans to do so. Are you planning to attend?"

"Actually, I am wondering if you really know who Mr. Zar is."

"What do you mean?"

"He is a man who thinks he is somebody, when he is actually nobody special. His following is small and he only seeks you to take advantage of your sister and her story to gain influence among the community."

"Well, that's an interesting accusation, but I'd like to know who you are before I put credence in it."

"I will not tell you who I am. I have nothing to gain in this transaction. I am only trying to convince you not to go with Mr. Zar because he has no following. A woman of your stature deserves better."

The caller spoke with an exceptionally pompous attitude. He was irritating me. "First of all, I am thankful to Mr. Zar for thinking of my sister and going to the trouble of arranging a service in her memory. Second, if you are not even willing to disclose your name, then what value can you expect me to place on your statement? Now, I have plenty to do right now and I've no desire to continue this discussion. Thank you and good-bye."

Once I put the phone down, I thought about how strange the caller was. He treated me like a pawn in somebody else's chess game.

The next day, I received a similar call from a man in Southern California. This gentleman was concerned about my engagement in Los Angeles.

"Ms. Darabi, I am Mr. Jamshid, and I want to first tell you that I'm very sorry for what your sister had to go through in her life. I was very touched when I heard of her demise. What is happening in our homeland is awful."

"Well, thank you. I'm glad to see that people have come to support her and her struggle."

"I have heard that you plan to speak at the memorial service held by Mr. Morovati. I want to convince you not to."

"May I ask why you feel that way?"

"Mr. Morovati and his followers are pro-shah. But a new monarch can offer our country little. We need to escape from this backward form of leadership to something more democratic."

"But, Mr. Jamshid, I am not a politician. I do not support any political movement in Iran. On the day of her death, my sister took a stand for human rights and that is all I am interested in supporting. I'll say that in my speech, too."

"Don't you see? They only want you in order for them to gain interest in their movement. It is the politics they are interested in. They're trying to take advantage of you." He paused for a little while.

"Well, Mr. Morovati has made a pleasant invitation to me, and I intend to go through with the appearance. I am not endorsing his movement by doing so and that will be made clear."

"Why don't you let me put something together? I own a few restaurants in Los Angeles. I can easily feed more than a thousand people. This way, you're in control of the service and no one takes advantage of you or your late sister."

I finally understood what he was up to. "Well sir, I will have to disappoint you. I don't plan to feed anyone. We will have a small gathering at my aunt's home the day before the service in Los Angeles, but I never planned to provide a caterer anywhere. I can't afford to feed a thousand people anyway."

His tone of voice changed, and I could sense that he was now disappointed. "Well," he said, "my colleagues and I would like the chance to meet you anyway. Please let us know when you plan to be in town and we'll have someone pick you up at the airport. We would appreciate an opportunity to accommodate you."

"That seems fair. I'll let you know as soon as I finalize my plans."

I called him the next day and gave him my travel plans. He said he needed to discuss the arrangements with his colleagues before he could commit to anything. He never called me back.

He must have thought that because my sister and I were both accomplished women, that I'd be willing to shell out a lot of money on some dinners in his restaurants. I guess when he realized I didn't plan on such an event, he didn't want to waste his time anymore.

Regardless, I attended services in Los Angeles as well as Portland, as planned, and things went smoothly in both cities.

Woman, mobilize!
and fight those who believe you are evil
when a strand of your hair is shown.
You are not tainted and there is no need to cover your face.
You are not a culprit and should not be chained.
Woman, there is no need for you,
as long as you are alive,
to submit to the one who believes
that you are nothing but his field of dreams.

This poem closed a memorial service for my sister that was held in Paris, France. It was written by Françoise D'Eaubonne and translated into Farsi by one of the ladies who organized the event.

I made it to Paris at about two in the afternoon. My host met me at the airport and brought me to her home so I could shower and change. We had to rush though, because the service was to start that evening and we had to meet some of the organizers before then.

People started arriving about thirty minutes after the scheduled start and the meeting began an hour late. It was a good meeting, though. I, two other speakers, and a translator sat together behind a table on a raised platform facing the audience. About two hundred people listened as I talked about my sister's life and a translator repeated the words in French, one paragraph at a time.

The meeting was well organized, and everything went smoothly. But what I will always remember about Paris is the people I met after the meeting. A woman from Algeria told me that she fled her country and came to France with her children because in Algeria, the Islamic fundamentalists were torturing and harassing women also.

An Iranian man also met with me. He said he was a member of the

Pan-Iranist political party. Apparently, I upset the gentleman by making a few statements about Dariush-e-Frouhar, the leader of the party.

"You know, I don't think you should suggest to people that your sister was not a member of our party when she died," he said.

"But sir, I'm only repeating what my sister told me. She said that after the Islamic revolution, Dariush became pro-Islamic and took a second wife. She told me she quit the party after that."

The gentleman held a newspaper clipping in his hands. "Look at this. This was published when my father died. It is a condolence note printed by many of your sister's colleagues, and her name is right here next to her husband's." He was pointing to a name printed in a condolence note. "See, Dr. Homa Darabi. She must have been a member."

I looked closely at the paper; Homa's name was on it. "Excuse me, but when did your father pass away?" I asked the man.

The man spoke softly. "He died recently, about a month ago."

"Well, sir, I'm sorry about your father, but given the condition my sister was in a month ago, I'm afraid she wouldn't have been able to publish a condolence note even if *I* died. Her husband must have done this on her behalf.

"Besides, nothing in this note says that these people belong to a party headed by Mr. Frouhar. I knew my sister well. I don't think she could ever follow a man with two wives."

I must have touched a nerve because he responded emphatically. "You know, people put too much emphasis on this matter. We all believe it was a mistake for Dariush to marry again. Still, he couldn't have done it without permission from his first wife, Parvaneh. She is a wonderful woman, and if she allowed him to take another wife, why should anyone else object? I mean, it's her husband!"

I couldn't walk away from this discussion. I was amazed by the nerve of the man standing before me. "Wait, are you telling me this was an insignificant mistake? Do you follow Dariush blindly?"

"I believe he could be a good leader for our country."

"Of course you do," I said. "You're a man! But what about the other half of the country? If he wanted a new wife he could have divorced his first, provided her with what was legally hers, and then given her the freedom to stay single or remarry.

"I don't understand how anyone can support a man that treats someone they love like nothing. What do you think women are? Are they like pairs of shoes in your political party? Is that why you need more than one?"

Eventually, I gave up on the conversation. It was getting late and I was exhausted after all the traveling.

From Paris, I flew to Germany for another meeting.

In Hamburg, as in Paris, my speech had to be translated. A man sat with me and recited my speech in German one paragraph at a time. The meeting here was in a small room and about seventy people were crowded into it.

I used the same transcript for each engagement. It included the fact that my sister was, at one time, a critic of the shah. This proved to be a sticking point with some listeners. Many of the people that fled Iran after the revolution were supporters of the shah and his father before him.

I guess a lot of people believed that my sister's fate was ironic because she spoke out against the Pahlavi dynasty and lived to suffer through a government that was more repressive to women than the shah and his father ever were.

The speaker who followed me seemed to see things this way. He was an old man. He focused most of his words on the reign of Reza Shah and his son, the king that followed.

"Reza Shah was a wonderful king. He believed in rebuilding Iran. He brought progress and prosperity to a backward country before he passed his dynasty down to his son, Mohammad Reza Shah. People like Homa Darabi could become doctors, engineers, or scientists because Reza Shah established schools and universities for them.

"But in time, these students turned on their leadership. They did not respect the value of what they were gaining and so they became dissenters. A visible kind of mutiny overcame our nation, and it was lost. Now it is a religious state, oppressive to any ideas outside the religious framework.

"We should all remember, now, that were it not for the work of Reza Shah and his son, there couldn't be professionals like Homa

Darabi. And let us not be so quick to criticize the dynasty that brought so much progress to our country."

Listening to him, I was very frustrated. He spoke like another blind follower. He seemed to suggest that simply because Reza Shah had brought positive things to Iran, his dynasty shouldn't be criticized for its mistakes.

I left for home with a bad taste in my mouth. Hamburg seemed as though it had been a waste of time.

The phone rang while I was working in my office one morning.

"Hello," It was a woman's voice, and she sounded young. "I am looking for Ms. Parvin Darabi?"

"This is she. May I help you?"

"I am calling from the office of Reza Shah the second. Please hold the line. His Majesty would like to speak with you."

"Sure."

I was surprised by the statement. Why would the son of the shah be calling me? I held the receiver for a few moments and then a man's voice came over the line.

"Ms. Darabi?"

"Yes?" I said.

"I'd like to extend my deepest condolences to you and your family for what must be an awful ordeal you are having to go through. I heard of your sister's passing when I was in Paris, and I wanted to call you from there, but I never found a chance. I just returned to my office in Washington. I wanted to take the first opportunity to call you and let you know how sorry I am."

"Thank you. That's kind of you to say."

"Please, Ms. Darabi, the next time you come to Washington, call my office and let me know. It would be nice to arrange some time to get together."

"I can do that. I travel to Washington pretty often. Thank you again for thinking about my sister. I do appreciate your kindness."

I sat there in my office, thinking about the conversation. He was so kind to reach out to me for the loss of my sister while not taking offense at any of her views. In that, he demonstrated more character than some of his followers had in the past few weeks. Still, I couldn't let go of the fact that my sister once held so much contempt for his family's monarchy. Was I betraying her by talking to him?

Later that afternoon, I got a call from a woman in Maryland who was distraught.

"Ms. Darabi, I just learned about your sister and what happened to her. Please accept my condolences."

Over the phone she started crying. With a broken voice, she described an ordeal her family had gone through after the revolution. She'd once been in charge of the department of customs in Iran, under the shah. After the revolt, she had to leave Iran to escape prosecution by revolutionary courts.

She was literally fleeing for her life. A few members of her family had already been executed by the Islamic Republic. She cried hard. For a moment I forgot all about my own loss and tried to comfort her. I tried to calm her down.

Calls like this one were endless. That evening, I talked to a mother whose nine-year-old daughter had complained about the rules of *hijab*. She'd written something that was declared to be an antiestablishment note. She was executed for that.

The mother told me that Khomeini responded to the prosecutor's question of whether the girl could be executed by saying, "The girl is nine years of age. She is considered an adult. She is ready to get married, pray, and fast in the holy month of Ramadan, therefore, she is also old enough to pay for her crime."

That story was especially disturbing. By the end, I was too distraught to talk to anyone else. I disconnected the ringer of my phone. I decided to light a fire in our living room and I went downstairs.

In the fireplace, I laid some kindling over a pile of lit paper. I kept adding paper to ignite the wood. I did this and watched the fire grow and then fade as the paper burned out. The wood blackened, but stubbornly. It would not burn. I fed it more paper and then decided to add some fresh wood. As I placed the log deep within the hearth, my middle finger touched a flame.

The pain made me jump back. My finger was sore, and I couldn't fight the tears. Suddenly, I felt sick about my sister. I thought of the pain she must have gone through as her entire body was enveloped in fire.

The thought made my stomach tighten. After a moment, I stepped back from the fireplace and sat on the couch before it. The fire burned brightly. The warmth reaching me brought back the memory of the *korsi* and the long winter nights when, as children, Homa and I waited for our father to come home and read to us. I think I would give anything to listen to him read us both one more story.

Index

273